A JOURNEY THROUGH
THE CYCLING YEAR

THE CYCLING PODCAST
RICHARD MOORE   LIONEL BIRNIE   DANIEL FRIEBE

A JOURNEY THROUGH THE CYCLING YEAR

YELLOW JERSEY PRESS
LONDON

1 3 5 7 9 10 8 6 4 2

Yellow Jersey Press, an imprint of Vintage
20 Vauxhall Bridge Road
London SW1V 2SA

Yellow Jersey Press is part of the Penguin Random House group of companies whose
addresses can be found at global.penguinrandomhouse.com.

Penguin
Random House
UK

First published by Yellow Jersey Press in 2018

www.vintage-books.co.uk

A CIP catalogue record for this book is available from the British Library

ISBN 9781787290266

Typeset in 11/15 pt FairfieldLH-Light by Jouve UK, Milton Keynes
Printed and bound by Clays Ltd, St Ives plc

Penguin Random House is committed to a sustainable future for
our business, our readers and our planet. This book is made from Forest
Stewardship Council® certified paper.

*To all our listeners and
friends of the podcast*

CONTENTS

CONTRIBUTORS

Lionel Birnie co-presents *The Cycling Podcast* having covered the sport since the late nineties. He co-founded *The Cycling Anthology* and ghost-wrote Sean Kelly's autobiography, *Hunger*.

Daniel Friebe co-presents *The Cycling Podcast* having written about cycling since the early 2000s. He is the author of *Mountain High* and *Mountain Higher* and *The Cannibal*, a biography of Eddy Merckx.

Richard Moore co-presents *The Cycling Podcast* and *The Cycling Podcast Féminin* and is the author of seven books, including *In Search of Robert Millar*, *Slaying the Badger* and *Étape*.

Ciro Scognamiglio is *The Cycling Podcast*'s favourite Italian and writes for *La Gazzetta dello Sport*.

Ashleigh Moolman Pasio, from South Africa, is one of the world's top cyclists. She was second in the 2016 Women's Tour and in 2016 and 2017 won the Giro della Toscana Femminile.

Sebastien Piquet is the voice of Radio Tour at the Tour de France and other major races.

François Thomazeau is the former head of sport at Reuters France, the author of several novels and non-fiction books, a musician (recording and performing as Sauveur Merlan), and the owner of a restaurant in Marseille and a bookshop in Paris. He first reported on the Tour de France in 1986.

Orla Chennaoui is a presenter on Sky Sports and co-hosts *The Cycling Podcast Féminin*.

Fran Reyes is a Spanish cycling journalist with tremendous sideburns and a fine singing voice.

Joe Dombrowski is an American professional cyclist who has ridden for Team Sky and Cannondale-Drapac.

1. A SORT-OF REVIEW OF THE CYCLING YEAR, PART 1

Richard Moore, Lionel Birnie and Daniel Friebe

RM: Where are we, Lionel?

LB: We're in London, in the British Film Institute Café, on a day when the sky has turned dark.

RM: Hurricane Ophelia. Is it a hurricane or a storm?

LB: Not sure. It started off as a hurricane, but it's fading . . .

RM: It's quite alarming, though. Feels apocalyptic. It feels like an appropriate sky under which to be discussing a sort-of review of the year.

LB: A review of cycling's last-ever season . . .

RM: My name's Richard Moore and I'm with Lionel Birnie . . .

LB: Hello, Richard.

RM: And Daniel Friebe.

DF: Hello.

RM: We are *The Cycling Podcast* team and we're returning to our roots. This is a sort of home fixture, isn't it, because over the years we've recorded a lot from the South Bank. Why did we start recording here? [long pause]

RM: Lucrative sponsorship deal with the National Theatre?

LB: No. Well, it was just a convenient meeting place when we first started. We're like travelling players, aren't we – we pitch up and podcast wherever . . .

DF: Mercenaries.

LB: This is kind of our home venue, our equivalent of The Globe, which is just along the South Bank here. This is where we feel at home.

RM: We do. I think because so much of our podcasting is at bike races, at Grand Tours, where you're forced by necessity to record wherever you can – it might be by some bins, or in a bar – we're used to improvising. I think we like to have a bit of background hubbub: coffee machines, people chatting in the background, people staring at you as they walk past because we're sitting here with microphones. So, anyway, this is the first *Cycling Podcast* book, a journey through the cycling year. It's by no means definitive, is it?

LB: Certainly not. What are we going to do? We're going to listen back to this then type it out and print it on paper? It's like the anti-podcast.

RM: It is. The whole point of podcasting is that it's supposed to be quite easy. We're making quite a lot of work for ourselves. I think the goal of the podcast has always been to focus on where we are rather than to try to cover everything. To take advantage of the fact that we are at races and speaking to some people, and try to bring a bit of the race to the listeners' ears, and this book is very much in the same vein. The idea is to take you, the listener (and now reader), through the cycling year. We'll begin where we started the year but we should maybe first do a bit of background into the podcast and into ourselves. We are journalists . . .

DF: [laughs] Sometimes.

RM: I think we can apply that term to what we do, can we not?

LB: I think the definition of a journalist has evolved and changed so much during the life of the podcast that we can still loosely attach that moniker to ourselves, can't we?

RM: We have covered the sport for quite a number of years. When was your first Tour de France, Daniel?

DF: 2001.

RM: You were the *benjamin*,* were you?

---

*   In the Bible, Benjamin was the twelfth and youngest son of Jacob (the eleventh was the more famous, technicolour dreamcoated Joseph), whose mother – Jacob's favourite wife – died during childbirth. Benjamin was much loved and mollycoddled (not a biblical term) by his father, who kept him at home rather than sending him away to Egypt

DF: I was. I was the youngest man at the Tour. I was younger than any rider by some distance, a couple of years, I think.

RM: 2001? Who was the youngest rider that year?

DF: That's a great question. I think it was . . . no, it wouldn't have been Philippe Gilbert. It was before his time. Was it David Moncoutié?* There was an oath that year, because we were already on about the third 'Tour of Renewal'. Every year when we started covering cycling there was a huge doping scandal that threatened to pull professional cycling under – and then it really would have been the last podcast, the last season, the last Tour, which seemed possible back then. Anyway, this was one of the 'Tours of Renewal'. It was supposed to relaunch the Tour de France, and there was a ceremonial oath about ethics and integrity read out on the start line of the first stage by the youngest rider in the race, and a white dove was released. That doesn't happen any more, does it? Do you not remember this?

RM: No, because my first Tour was 2005. Lionel, you were covering it then . . .

LB: Yeah, I was at the first of the modern Tours of Renewal . . .

DF: I thought you were going to say you were at the first Tour then. At the *Réveil Matin* . . .

LB: I was. And I remember saying to Henri Desgrange, 'This is going to be quite tough, isn't it? How am I going to get to Lyon?' No, my first Tour was the 1999 Tour. I did about a week of it and I thought I knew about cycling before then. I'd been a journalist for quite a few years but it was my first full year as a cycling journalist. I'd been to a few races before but being parachuted into the Tour midway through . . . everything I thought I knew about cycling at that point turned out to be wrong, really. It was the most bewildering event. And I think even now, what, eighteen years later . . .

_____

with his brothers, though he did eventually join them. At the Tour de France, the youngest rider in the race is known as Benjamin.

* It was Sylvain Chavanel, born in June 1979.

RM: It's still bewildering.

LB: Still bewildering, exactly. Rich, this year we travelled with François Thomazeau whose first Tour was in 1986 and even he is still grasping at bits of it. There are still corners of the Tour that are a slight mystery to him. You never quite got to grips with it all, because – this is a bit metaphorical – the Tour's always moving along so it's continually moving away from you. Just when you get comfortable, you all have to get up and move on again. I think that's why the Grand Départ is always so bewildering – because you do start to feel comfortable in one place for two or three days and it hasn't even got started, then the whole show sort of picks up and moves on. Then you can extrapolate the way the Tour works to the whole cycling season: it's a massive travelling roadshow that kicks off every year . . . well, the World Tour kicks off in Australia and then goes to the Middle East, after which we all get excited about the cobbled Classics in the spring, and it runs on parallel train tracks, doesn't it, because while we're excited about the cobbled Classics the Grand Tour riders are also doing Paris–Nice or Tirreno–Adriatico or the Volta a Catalunya or Tour of the Basque Country. There's always something to keep your eyes on, and, before you know where you are, we've got our heads down and we're going towards the Tour of Flanders, Paris–Roubaix, the big Monuments . . . It never stays still.

RM: So '99 was the first Tour you worked at, Lionel. What was the first Tour you ever saw in the flesh?

LB: Ooh, in the flesh would be '97. Yeah.

RM: Quite late.

LB: Yeah. When it came to Britain in '94 I wasn't allowed time off from the newspaper I worked at. Basically, I'd just come back from a training course and you're supposed to do six months without any holiday. They wouldn't allow this now; these were inhumane working conditions! I couldn't even take a couple of days off to go down to Portsmouth or Brighton, where it came over for a couple of days in 1994. So the first time I set eyes on the Tour was in '97, I think I'm right in saying. I'd seen other races before but not the Tour de France.

RM: Where did you see it in 1997?

LB: Saint-Étienne. The time-trial that went over the Col de la République. I remember that because there were some Italian fans who were singing sort of football songs for all of their riders. Francesco Casagrande, Marco Pantani . . . They were handing around a bottle of grappa as well. They were on one side of the road and on the other side of the road, just up from where my dad and I were standing, there was a very well-dressed woman – late middle-aged, I'd say – and she had a cat in a basket. This is absolutely true – every time a French rider came past, she lifted the cat up in its basket and kind of showed the cat the rider. The cat got very excited when Richard Virenque went past, I can tell you.

RM: Daniel, when was the first Tour you saw?

DF: 1998. I was working on a golf course in France that summer and I went to the start of the stage the morning after Festina got kicked out of the race. It started in Montauban. I can't remember where it finished but Jacky Durand won the stage in a breakaway.*

LB: I thought Daniel was going to say that he'd been doing work experience with the Gendarmerie and that he'd been along to arrest Virenque and Alex Zülle . . .

RM: All Daniel's interests colliding there – the golf course and the bicycling. I'm a bit older than you guys, of course, so my first Tour was 1990. It was also my first trip abroad. I was seventeen! No budget airlines in those days! We were on holiday in Annecy and the Tour went nearby. We rode to Albertville and watched it on a climb. I don't actually know which climb it was.† The stage finished halfway up Mont Blanc.‡ We waited for a long time. We got there very early – I

---

* This is incorrect: Jacky Durand had won the previous day in Montauban. Leon van Bon won the stage from Montauban to Pau.

† In fact, the Moores didn't ride, they drove. And they didn't go to Albertville: the stage climbed the Colombière and Aravis, neither very close to Albertville. It was the next day that Richard rode to Albertville to watch the race pass.

‡ Astonishingly, this is correct.

was just with my dad and my brother – and we watched on the climb as Thierry Claveyrolat came through on his own. He was an RMO rider. I remember the Ray-Bans. Of course, no helmets in those days. He had a very distinctive style. We were standing with some French supporters who all thought it was Charly Mottet because he was the team leader at RMO. I corrected them and my dad was very proud and surprised that I seemed to know more than these French fans. I can still see it in my mind's eye. I can still remember what Thierry Claveyrolat looked like. He was from very nearby and is dead now sadly, having committed suicide several years later, after his life had sort of unravelled in retirement . . . But he was a very stylish and exciting climber. I can still see him riding past, and I can still see Greg LeMond behind him in his world champion's jersey and his Scott bars that continued across the bottom to give him an aero position. Robert Millar was there, his Z teammate, Gianni Bugno . . . It's amazing how vivid that first sighting is and how it lodges itself in your brain.

LB: I'd been watching races for so long on TV, since the early eighties, really, because it had been broadcast on Channel 4, but there was something about it that captured me immediately. It wasn't as though I gradually got interested. It was a sport that was so visually arresting that I wanted to know more and more about it. Certainly in those days it wasn't that easy to learn about how the whole sport operated. It was a long, meandering journey whereby I read lots of things that informed but also misled me. There are myths about the sport that are still lodged in my brain that I can't dislodge, like the famous old one about Bernard Hinault winning Paris–Roubaix once and never riding it again, which is actually wrong. I think I read that somewhere . . .

RM: I think it was in *Slaying The Badger*, first edition! The myth came from Hinault himself, who said it in an interview, or it was mistranslated in an interview . . . Daniel, did your love of cycling, if I can call it that . . .

DF: Tolerance of cycling!

RM: Did your mild interest in cycling not owe something to your interest in languages?

DF: Yeah, I would say so. At that point in my mid-teens my golf career was already going awry. My dad was quite a pushy parent, I think it's fair to say. Even when he plays golf with me now he gets in a mood if I don't play well. I'm in my mid-thirties, by the way . . . So, yeah, I think I was subconsciously looking for something that my dad wasn't interested in. I'd also been to France on holiday, been to Italy on holiday, and the only thing I was any good at in school was languages. I was very passionate about languages, and the two things . . . cycling seemed like this secret code that needed to be cracked, and one of the ways to crack it was by speaking French, or Spanish, or Italian or Dutch. So I latched onto it. I also loved the mountains. It's difficult to pinpoint exactly when I first sat down and watched a stage of the Tour de France and was absolutely captivated but I can remember glimpses, being on holiday in France and seeing Pascal Lino on TV. That could have been 1992 possibly. This vague awareness of Indurain dominating the sport. Then 1996 was the first Tour that I watched in any great detail. I can certainly remember watching the stage to Les Arcs, which ended up being one of the stages of the decade because so much happened that day. Stéphane Heulot started that stage in the yellow jersey and climbed off and abandoned on the summit of the Cormet de Roselend; you had Johan Bruyneel going off the side of a road and into a ravine; and Miguel Indurain cracked, which just seemed like this incredible watershed. Even I, who had no real depth of understanding of the context, could appreciate what a huge moment this was, that Indurain, this sort of unbreakable robot, had finally been cracked, and no one could quite believe it. After that I was very much infatuated with it quite quickly.

LB: Do you not think that one of the charms of cycling, even now, is this awkward marriage between tradition and innovation? As Daniel was talking there about the 1992 Tour, where Pascal Lino was almost the breakthrough rider, had the yellow jersey, and you were thinking that maybe he was going to be . . .

RM: Looked incredible on a bike. Very stylish.

LB: And every year, because of the way we consumed the Tour particularly – at twelve-month intervals, really – you had to work quite hard to piece together the rest of the cycling season. Very often, if I'd read about Pascal Lino, for example, I wouldn't have seen any footage in the UK of him actually racing. But I remember that 1992 Tour – because they were celebrating the European Community, the EEC, they visited all the countries that bordered France, so Belgium, the Netherlands – I know that doesn't quite border France . . .

DF: Started in San Sebastián, didn't it?

LB: Started in San Sebastián, in the Basque Country in northern Spain.

RM: The Channel 4 car was bombed by Basque separatists on the eve of the race.

LB: That's right, yeah. But what struck me when I first saw the route and realised they'd be going into the Pyrenees on about day two, only a day or so after the prologue, was that it was the first time I'd been unsettled and bamboozled by the Tour de France. In my mind that was not supposed to happen: you were supposed to have nine or ten days of the race before the mountains. It unsettled me. And I think as we look at the way the races have evolved in recent years and continue to evolve, there's always a sense of uncomfortableness about things that are too different and veer too far from tradition while on the other hand the sport is desperately trying to innovate and create new events. I'm thinking about the Hammer Series, for example, which is really ripping up what we think we know about road racing and trying to inject something different into it.

RM: It's interesting that Daniel talks about languages. Even those of us who are not quite as proficient in languages as Daniel is . . . it's still one of those things that attracted me to the sport, because it did add an air of mystery and intrigue and indecipherability, I suppose, that keeps me interested. One of the ways the sport is trying to move forward and change is by embracing the English language. Certainly since we started the English language has become ubiquitous in professional cycling, which makes our jobs easier on one hand but on the other you feel the sport has lost something, especially when you see

Italian teams with English slogans on the side of the bus.* Also at the Giro itself you hear a lot of English – the official commentary and so on – and to me that's not what the Giro should be.

LB: It's another example of the contradictions that exist within professional road racing: the desire to be an international sport and yet you go to certain pockets and it's incredibly parochial. You go to the Belgian Classics, the Flemish Classics, and there'll be as big a crowd around the bus of a Belgian Continental division team as there will be . . . I mean, some of the big teams are completely ignored because they don't have any Belgian riders. They'll be getting ready almost in anonymity. In a region like Flanders, particularly, there's such an identification with their heroes. Eventually they warm to people from the outside, but you have to do something special in their races. Peter Sagan, for example, could win the Tour de France but it's winning the Tour of Flanders and the world title that makes him a star here. There are sorts of tiers and layers of acceptance in places like that and other places too.

DF: I think it's easy to forget how quickly the globalisation has happened. We've mentioned this before particularly when analysing performances and determining the reasons why in real or gross terms performances have improved or, well, kept pace with what we consider to be the disgraced performances of the 1990s. The gene pool has become so much wider and can get a lot wider still. We see smatterings of riders from all over the world now but it's not as cosmopolitan as other sports, football for example. That said, you compare it to twenty years ago and you see how much more international it is. You look back at the era we're talking about, the mid-nineties, and the Giro would have seventeen Italian teams out of twenty. Italian riders generally wouldn't do the

---

* English is everywhere, usually in the form of naff hashtags such as #KeepPushing or #NeverGiveUp, though the funniest example was perhaps when some Italian pros had temporary tattoos which said: 'I'm doping free.' We knew what they meant, but they could easily be misinterpreted as 'I'm doping *for* free.'

Tour in the late-nineties or early nineties. That's been one major change since we all started following it, I think . . .

RM: We were going to kick off by talking about where we started our season, and Daniel you did go to one of the new races in one of the new territories.

DF: Yeah, I was at the Abu Dhabi Tour. First time I'd been to any of the Gulf races, which have been around for well over ten years now. From a racing point of view, it wasn't particularly thrilling but what it did do was set up what I thought was going to be a real ding-dong, a great battle in 2017 between the established powers in sprinting – Cavendish, Kittel and Greipel – and the emerging talents, or particularly Caleb Ewan, given that he was there and Gaviria was not. Looking back now on the year in its entirety that was a slight disappointment; we've spoken before about how this rivalry, or what had the potential to be a fantastic rivalry between Cavendish and Kittel, has never really crackled into life. It's almost been a case of shadow-boxing for several years, during which their best periods have not coincided. In Abu Dhabi I think they had one stage win each and Ewan had one, too. So everything was shaping up for that duel to happen between Cavendish and Kittel in particular, but Cavendish ended up having a really poor season, for health reasons primarily. He had the Epstein–Barr virus early in the season then he crashed at the Tour de France. That's actually one of the enduring disappointments of the last few seasons in professional cycling for me – that it's been such a moveable feast and changeable cast of characters in that particular discipline of sprinting. It's a part of cycling that lends itself to rivalries but we've not really seen them too much in the last few years.

RM: Where did you start your season, Lionel?

LB: The first race I did was Omloop Het Nieuwsblad, which was a sort of *hors d'oeuvre* before the Lionel of Flanders.

RM: How could we forget the Lionel of Flanders? A series of podcasts you did for Friends of the Podcast in the spring really getting under the skin of the lesser-known Flanders Classics.

LB: Yeah, the races that build up to the Tour of Flanders, so that's the Dwars Door Vlaanderen, the Grand Prix E3 Harelbeke and Ghent–Wevelgem, all of which have a very similar but distinct character and there's a story behind each of them.

RM: They are a precursor to the big cobbled Classics – the Tour of Flanders and Paris–Roubaix – but was there anything that you saw there that had an impact on the bigger races to come?

LB: Well, Philippe Gilbert got into the winning break at Dwars Door Vlaanderen with Yves Lampaert of Quick-Step, the eventual winner. There was another Quick-Step rider in there too . . . Who was that? [Pause] Oh, of course, it was Philippe Gilbert!

RM: He was wearing the Belgian champion's jersey, though . . .

LB: Ah, yes, that's right, because in my mind's eye I could see them going past on the cobbles but I couldn't remember who the second Quick-Step rider was. That's the advantage of transcribing this conversation for the book. We can cut all this out.* Anyway, Gilbert was second at Dwars Door Vlaanderen and at the Grand Prix E3 Harelbeke and then he went on and absolutely crushed the Tour of Flanders. It was sort of Fabian-Cancellara-at-Paris–Roubaix-esque wasn't it? The Tour of Flanders was also notable for the crash where Peter Sagan caught a flag or a bag . . .

RM: It was a jacket.

LB: That's right, it was a jacket. It was on the Oude Kwaremont at a crucial time in the race. Gilbert had already gone away and Sagan was in this chasing group with Greg Van Avermaet and Oliver Naesen and he was riding extremely close to the barriers to try to avoid the cobbles. They had to try to keep that gap close. Sagan was hugging the barriers, he caught his handlebars and he went down and Van Avermaet went down as well. Van Avermaet had won Harelbeke and Ghent–Wevelgem . . .

RM: And he went on to win Paris–Roubaix . . .

LB: The Tour of Flanders hinged on those two moments – Gilbert's attack and the Sagan crash – and the great unknown is whether Gilbert would

---

* No, we can't.

have stayed away had that crash not happened. In ten or fifteen years' time when we look back and review the decade's Classics, Gilbert's performance will be one we look back at as a crushing performance and it will be forgotten, perhaps, that he was considerably aided by the fact that powerful chasing group all hit the deck.

RM: I read a fascinating interview with Gilbert recently where he talked about his strategy, with being away on his own like that with so long to go. He said he didn't just ride it as a time trial, flat out, he knew the wind conditions and the roads so he was able to give himself a bit of an easy ride at certain points but, when he knew they would be chasing hard behind, he would hit the gas a bit because he knew that psychologically if the chasers were riding hard and not closing the gap, they would be broken. I mean, on paper three men chasing one guy, when the differences between them are minute, you think, how can it be that they can't close the gap, but the difference is that the chasers are having to measure their effort in a way that the one rider up front isn't. And so, the riders behind are not necessarily riding flat out. They are playing a game too, because they are doing as much as they think they need to do while also holding something back in the event that the leader is caught and they get a chance to go for the win.

DF: It was a major resurgence for Gilbert. A lot of people had written him off and he was maybe unfairly bracketed with other riders who had gone to BMC and found themselves in a bit of a comfort zone, getting paid a lot of money and experiencing a downturn in results. He'd certainly had that downturn in results when he went to BMC but everything you hear from guys around the peloton suggests that he's always been a very hard worker and he continued to work hard but what didn't suit him at BMC was more the style of racing. BMC are quite prescriptive about how their leaders ride – or they have been in the past – surrounded by *domestiques* all the time, with not that much room for improvisation, and that is Gilbert's strength. That very prescribed style of racing is definitely not his strength and Quick-Step enabled him to go back to his roots as a real racer, I think, and he seemed to revel in that. Part of that was that he was able to do the Tour of Flanders, which he'd had to skip for a few years because Van Avermaet was in the same team at BMC.

RM: He was at BMC for five years, potentially his best years, his early thirties. He's not had the sort of results during his time at BMC that he had in his last year before he joined them, or this year, when he's been phenomenal, so you wonder how many riders are in teams, or have roles within teams, which don't suit them.

LB: So, Rich, where did the Buffalo start his season?

RM: The Buffalo trotted off to Paris–Nice, primarily to talk to Mat Hayman about his win at Paris–Roubaix in 2016 for a Friends of the Podcast special episode. That was really great because it was a chance to do something that we don't often get a chance to do and that's sit and watch a race with a rider as they talk through how it happened. I think it was your idea, wasn't it, Lionel?

LB: [nods]

RM: At Paris–Nice I did a few other interviews. On the first night I bumped into Richie Porte, who had been following the story with his former team, Team Sky, over the winter, and felt aggrieved because he felt some of the coverage and various controversies had been, in his words, sensationalised and he was very keen to give us an interview and explain what he thought about Team Sky with the Bradley Wiggins TUEs and so on. His team, BMC, weren't too keen for him to sit down and talk about Team Sky and their woes, they wanted him to focus on BMC but he went off-piste and spoke his mind, as Richie Porte often does.

It was an interesting race for Porte because he had started the season very well and as the season went on he showed that he could go to the Tour de France as a real contender. What was interesting for him at Paris–Nice was the strength of Team Sky. The theme of the season was that [the controversies] didn't seem to affect them, from Strade Bianche and Milan–San Remo with Michal Kwiatkowski, and Sergio Henao at Paris–Nice, then Chris Froome winning the Tour de France and the

Vuelta a España, they had their best-ever season. They looked really formidable.

At the other end, there was Cannondale-Drapac, who I spent quite a bit of time with at Paris–Nice because I was booked into the same hotels as them. It was interesting observing their body language at breakfast because there was almost a sense within the team of defeat. You could even pick it up at breakfast. Riders who normally are quite cheerful and upbeat were shuffling in, not making eye contact and looking at their feet. I did speak to some of the riders and they did say that there was a sense within the team that things were not going right. At that point they had not won a World Tour race for a year-and-a-half and they would not win one until May at the Tour of California and then of course at the Giro d'Italia with Pierre Rolland. But it was really palpable that feeling of a team that was in a downward spiral and the ultimate metaphor was that during Paris–Nice their bus broke down and they ended the race in a white mini-van with windows and seats. Watching the riders in Nice getting changed out the back of a car, it was . . .

LB: Old school.

RM: It was but you felt this was a team really at rock-bottom and, coincidentally or not, it was a team that almost went out of existence but there was a sense that this was a team that was really on their uppers.

LB: You mentioned Cannondale as a team that struggled to get results for a long time but the one thing that stood out for me during the spring particularly was the concentration of power in the hands of so few teams. When you look at the races from January up to the Tour de Romandie in late April, early May, which is the last of the spring races before the Grand Tours get underway, Richie Porte of BMC won the two stage races that book-end that period, that's the Tour Down Under and the Tour de Romandie. His BMC teammate Greg Van Avermaet dominated the cobbled Classics, although Quick-Step also had some success there with Gilbert winning the Amstel Gold race as well. In the Ardennes, Alejandro Valverde of Movistar won both Flèche Wallonne and Liège–Bastogne–Liège – he also won three big stage races and then

Team Sky made it four teams that really dominated the entire spring. Back twenty or thirty years ago it wouldn't be too surprising if a few teams or riders dominated to such an extent but I think now, with the diversity and supposed strength-in-depth in the peloton, I think it tells us something about the concentration of wealth and talent in relatively few teams and when those teams and riders get on a roll they can win a lot of races in succession and dominate certain phases of the season.

RM: It also links somewhat to the point I was making about riders in teams and roles that may not suit them, conversely you see teams with different line-ups riding in the same way and winning. I was thinking of stage 2 of the Vuelta, to Grand Narbonne, with the crosswinds. Yves Lampaert won the stage for Quick-Step, Matteo Trentin helped set it up. It was almost identical to what Quick-Step did at stage 3 of the Giro but with entirely different riders. I think about this in relation to team time trials as well, where a different line-up representing BMC or Quick-Step or Orica or Sky, can finish in the top four for every team time trial in a Grand Tour. And that is interesting too, there's a DNA in a team that means a different cast of riders can produce identical results because they ride in a certain way.

RM: For this book, we have written diaries about the three Grand Tours which tell the story of the journey we are on as much as the race itself but the Giro this year was much anticipated because it was the 100th Giro . . .

DF: I thought you were going to say because the food's great . . .

RM: There's that as well. The food is wonderful, isn't it. This year the Giro was entirely on Italian soil, starting in Sardinia and finishing in Milan. Daniel, did the Giro do what the 100th Giro would have set out to do?

DF: As a race it took a lot of time to get going but this is increasingly the way the major tours are going because the organisers are trying to stack as much of the action towards the back as possible. At the same time, we think, and we have seen over the last few years, we hope that because of the way cycling has cleaned itself up, the riders don't have as many bullets, or as powerful an armoury, as they used to have in terms of attacks and in terms of the energy they can expend. They tend to try to keep their powder dry for as long as possible in order to put in what are going to be decisive attacks. That often means waiting until the last couple of stages. It was pretty cagey until the last few stages. That was maybe a slight flaw in the way the course was designed. I think Mauro Vegni, the director of the Giro, is slightly undecided in the same way that Christian Prudhomme and the Tour de France are slightly undecided about the way to go. Do they fully embrace short, spectacular stages, what you might consider gimmicky stages, or do they stay faithful to the traditions and heritage of the race? Not just in a sporting sense but the Grand Tours are supposed to represent a journey and provide a snapshot of a country. I am not entirely sure they are clear on that yet. The Grand Tour that has the strongest identity at the moment is the Vuelta because it seems to know exactly what it is and what it wants to do and is very confident about the direction it wants to go in.

So at the Giro we had Quintana, Pinot, Dumoulin and Nibali battling it out for almost the entirety of the three weeks and there were various points when it looked like any one of them could have won. Dumoulin was a surprise, though. He came into the season being quite cagey, as he has been for the past couple of years, always under-promising but over-delivering. He was saying he wanted to be top five or top ten and then he goes and contends for the win. We gave his team Sunweb a bit of flak – we weren't alone in suggesting that his team was not particularly powerful in that race. They had come in with quite an inexperienced team but because there were so many riders in conten-tion, Dumoulin was able to use those other teams too, by surfing the wheels and taking advantage of the work the other teams were doing and the lack of a strong team did not become a major issue for him until very late in the race, the last couple of days, and by that point he was home and dry.

LB: You mention the Giro showcasing the country, because I did the first two weeks from Sardinia to Sicily then across the bridge of the foot to the heel and then snaking up the middle to Bergamo in the north. What struck me about that journey was how gradually Italy changes. Every day felt like yesterday but if you thought back three or four days it felt like a slightly different country. So by the time we got north it had crept up on me how much Italy had changed. It struck me the people were friendlier in the south. They were sunnier and more gregarious in the south. Sicily was obviously terrifying because I thought the mafia were lurking round every corner and might take an interest in our gleaming white Maserati* and think we were big-time players or something. The food was also much better in the south.

DF: That's a *big* call! We could do an hour-long podcast on just that topic. The food is much better in the south?

LB: I think so, yes. I think the quality and simplicity. It's much less pretentious. In the north there's a sort of culinary complacency . . .

DF: As you inch closer to France, it gets more complacent . . .

LB: We were unfortunate when we reached Bergamo because I was looking forward to a traditional dish of polenta but we had been invited for a pizza by the Giro's press office people so we missed out on that.

DF: Lionel's got a mental filing cabinet of every meal he's had.

RM: I bet you couldn't tell us who won the stage that day.

LB: I could actually because it was Bob Jungels but I remember that because the winner's press conference was in the Bergamo chamber of commerce or something and the room we were in had this amazing stained-glass image on the ceiling, with the light coming through, and that stuck in my mind.

Anyway, back to the Giro. I don't want to pollute the podcast book with a football analogy but Sunweb were like Leicester City when they won the Premier League. Every day in the mountains we expected it

---

* Maserati were kind enough to supply *The Cycling Podcast* with a beautiful white Quattroporte for the Giro. It was gleaming when we collected it.

to be the day when Sunweb fell apart but it didn't happen. They didn't have the strongest collection of individuals but when they worked together they used their resources very well. One of my last stages on the Giro was the one to Oropa, another stunning climb with a beautiful monastery up there, and obviously famous for Marco Pantani's heroics back in the Nineties. That was the day when Dumoulin won, when everyone had expected others to put him on the back foot, but what was striking to me was how tight-knit the Sunweb group was. The first few riders waited for the last ones before setting off back down to where the team bus was parked so they could all have a little moment of celebration together. That was the moment when I started to think that Dumoulin might be able to do it.

DF: I think [Sunweb are] really good at making targets but also setting long-term plans, often plans that go beyond the length of riders' contracts. With Dumoulin a couple of years ago they had been talking about a four-year plan or a five-year plan to get him ready to contend in major tours. Just to broaden it out, the question about teams, it's a theme not only in the Giro but how important are teams at the Grand Tours? There's such a high premium now on not just winning Grand Tours but pretty much any position in the top ten. So the old canons about the responsibility to work falling on the team of the race leader, or the rider who is highest up the general classification, does often not apply now because there will always be someone who will take it on themselves to pull. We've seen it numerous times in recent years where there's been a dangerous move down the road and a few guys have looked at each other as if to say, which team is going to pull? And there will always be a team that will pull and so guys [race leaders] who do not have a particularly strong team have often got away with it.

LB: As it was the 100th Giro, Rich, you started by asking whether it was what the country of Italy and the race organisers would have wanted as a great celebration of the race, well, they had only one stage win and they had to wait two weeks for it before Vincenzo Nibali won in Bormio. Nibali was third overall and didn't really ever look like repeating the last-week heroics of 2016 but he gave it a reasonable shot at times. No days in the pink jersey either for Italian riders. It was a race that celebrated Italy but didn't necessarily celebrate Italian cycling.

DF: Can I throw in something, gratuitously, that I found out the other day about Italians and the pink jersey? In 1971 the Giro started with a team relay race and Vincenzo Torriani the race boss decided that all the riders in the winning team should wear the pink jersey the next day. It was Salvarani, Gimondi's team.

LB: I think I did know that.

RM: For me one of the big surprises, perhaps *the* surprise of the season, was that the Hammer Series got a pretty positive response from us.

LB: I was dead against it. I don't like anything new.

RM: Oddly, you do like the idea of innovation but the reality of this, I wasn't sure . . . one would almost think you'd had cocktails in the desert with . . .

DF: . . . Graham Bartlett.*

LB: I think I'm the only one of us who hasn't had cocktails with Graham Bartlett.

RM: I haven't.

LB: No, I think it was good to see something new. Last year we made an episode looking, well, only three years into the future [laughs]. You don't need a very big crystal ball for that, do you. How will cycling look in 2020?

RM: What were we thinking?

LB: It was the kind of woolly thinking the UCI calendar department are sometimes guilty of. But now the Hammer Series is underway, on the one hand it's asking a question that nobody's really asked: what does road racing need other than stage racing and one-day racing? And yet when you look at the whole menu of races on the World Tour, it's clear there is room for some kind of innovation. Certainly the hilly Hammer Series

---

* Chief executive of Velon, who organise the Hammer Series.

stage, won by Carlos Betancur, was a great watch. It was like Twenty20 cricket. The action was condensed into under two hours. It was exciting.

RM: The team time trial was a great watch as well.

LB: Um, yes it was, but by accident rather than design, with the coming together of the teams at the finish, they were lucky . . .

DF: Not sure about that. I think the nature of it will dictate that a lot of them are like that, because of the nature of the pursuit . . .

LB: Well it's designed to be like that to, to come down to . . .

RM: So you've contradicted yourself there. You said accident rather than design. And we've done the equivalent of waiting in a doorway, with leg outstretched, and watched you fall flat on your face . . .

LB: I meant they got lucky in the sense that it could have been a right mess, it could have been a shambles, but actually there was an element of pursuit to it . . .

DF: It could've been like that scene in *Anchorman* when the four news crews fight in the courtyard . . .

LB: But it was an entertaining watch. The sprint stage didn't work at all, the bunch didn't stay together, it broke up and became like a classic-lite.

DF: Was that not interesting in itself?

LB: It was a terrible-looking course, round a cycle park – the Tom Dumoulin cycle park – but there wasn't enough in that sprint stage to make you think, that's worth sitting down to watch . . .

RM: We went from there to the Dauphiné and saw a great race, partly because riders are prepared to be more adventurous and take more risks at the Dauphiné than they do at the Tour. Jakob Fuglsang won and on the last day Richie Porte appeared to be ganged up on. We went to the Tour with no real sense of Froome as the outstanding favourite because he hadn't won a race and he fell apart a bit on the final day of the Dauphiné. It looked very open until . . . the first day, in Düsseldorf.

LB: Geraint Thomas won the prologue and for a while it looked like Sky might have the yellow jersey from start to finish. But for Aru's couple of days in yellow, it was perfect for Sky. I think it's a reminder that conservative racing often pays dividends. Froome manoeuvred his way around the Tour de France without having to be extra special but without really making too many mistakes.

RM: He did what he needed to do.

LB: Despite saying beforehand [the course] wasn't ideal for him I think it was pretty much ideal for him because he got himself in front early thanks to La Planche des Belles Filles and he more or less stayed there all the way to Paris, plotting his way around France.

RM: Plotting is the word. He went on to the Vuelta. You felt it was a box he needed to tick, a scratch that needed to be itched. It's surprising, certainly in the modern era, since Greg LeMond, that a winner of the Tour de France would try to win a second Grand Tour. I mean, Indurain did it winning the Giro but you felt that was part of his preparation to try and win the Tour. Since then nobody, with the exception of Marco Pantani, has won two Grand Tours in the same year, or even tried. Lance Armstrong, if we can call him a Tour winner, never tried to win a second Grand Tour in a season, and nobody else has. Perhaps only Carlos Sastre in 2008 went reasonably close.

DF: Contador? When he won the Giro and the Vuelta in 2008?

RM: I'm talking about the Tour. Nobody has tried to win a second Grand Tour as well as the Tour.

DF: Contador did try in 2011.

RM: He went nowhere near.

DF: But he did try!

LB: It's like you've been tripped up by a doorframe with nobody even standing there.

RM: I've tripped myself up. The point is that Froome did not *need* to go and win the Vuelta. In terms of what was in it for him, financially or by any other measure, there was only sporting ambition.

LB: How quaint that sporting ambition has any currency in the professional era.

RM: You had the sense he was there trying to win the Vuelta because he wanted to win the Vuelta. I thought that was very impressive and I admired him for it.* The Vuelta is in many ways harder to win than the Tour. There were no sprinters, so there were no sprinters' teams controlling certain stages. Every single stage had something to concern him. He had to be 'on' it every stage, a very difficult thing to do. He had one wobble the day after the time trial but he looked pretty in control and he took the red jersey on day three, into Andorra. The race was close but as with the Tour that closeness . . .

LB: It didn't mean suspense, did it, in either race . . . Going back to what you said about the DNA of teams and seeing teams racing in a certain way regardless of the personnel at the race, I think Team Sky is an absolutely classic example of that. If you go back to 2016 – I'm not saying Chris Froome took the Vuelta lightly and thought that all he needed to do was climb well and he would win – I think the team's approach was too footloose and fancy free. This year they rode the Vuelta like the Tour de France. They executed the same plan with a different line-up of riders and Froome took it extremely seriously right from the start, rather than hoping to get in a good position and follow wheels up the GC, he seized the initiative early, banked his advantage when he was still strong from the Tour de France, and then, I don't think he did fade, he did have a little wobble at the beginning of the final week, but he had enough in the bank that he could see Madrid coming towards him. It was never really out of his control.

DF: I think there were times this summer when it looked as though Froome's dynasty was reaching its plateau and he'd reached this phase that riders reach when they have won multiple Grand Tours, Tours de France in particular, and they start to ride more conservatively. They can't do the big attacks any more, just enough. We thought Froome had definitely reached that stage. I think maybe in hindsight we should have

---

* We are talking before the news broke in December 2017 of Chris Froome's adverse analytical finding for salbutamol, the asthma medication permitted up to a certain threshold. The Froome case – he had double the limit in a test taken after stage 18 of the Vuelta – remained unresolved when this book went to press.

For captions, see page 243

looked at the Tour de France as part one of a two-part objective. He wasn't as strong at the Tour de France because his focus was equally on the Vuelta. I was struck at the Dauphiné by how confident Froome was, and how confident Nicolas Portal, his DS at Sky, was about the Tour. He didn't seem to have that edge, that extra zip, but I think he rode ... well, everything went exactly according to plan, the way his form evolved over nine, ten weeks between the start of the Tour and the end of the Vuelta. Maybe he didn't hit the highs he has done in previous years but I don't think that's necessarily a sign that he's teetered over the plateau and he'll be an easier target next year. The other thing that could have beaten him at the Tour was a rival more willing to go for broke and really gamble everything. We talked at the Tour de France about podium positions, and top 10 positions, are so prestigious now for riders and teams – and there were a lot of riders at the Tour de France for whom a podium or top 10 was a career-changing result. It was worth half a million, a million on their contract next year, and we see that more and more.

LB: Yeah and the only rider who was willing and able to make that gamble was Mikel Landa, his teammate. We're looking forward to Landa going to Movistar and riding in tandem with Nairo Quintana, we imagine. Will he be in service to Quintana or able to race for himself? Being the second-best rider in a team with the [yellow] jersey gives you a lot of confidence and freedom because nothing rested on him. He looked as fresh as a daisy on some of these climbs but the team's fortunes didn't rest on Mikel Landa, so there's a bubble of security around him that none of these other riders in the top ten have got.

RM: It's like a lead-out man going to become a sprinter somewhere else, and invariably it doesn't work out ...

DF: I think people have been very naïve about that in the past, looking at the second best, or Sky's best *domestique*, thinking that guy will go off and challenge Froome. We've seen it with Richie Porte; OK, he's got there in the end, he can cause Froome problems, but he hasn't done it over three weeks. Geraint Thomas, we haven't seen it from him yet.

Wout Poels rode some outstanding stages at the Vuelta but has never finished anywhere close to the podium in a Grand Tour. I think Landa could threaten Froome but it's no foregone conclusion.

RM: Kwiatkowksi caught a lot of people's eyes for his performances at the Tour, but it's a totally different proposition if your finish line is half way up the mountain.

LB: Indeed. Is it coffee time yet?

RM: Oh, a flat white, please.

DF: [rolls eyes]

2. THE LIONEL OF FLANDERS

Lionel Birnie

An A to Z of the lesser-known cobbled Classics

I was on the phone to one of our producers, Tom Whalley, explaining my idea for a series of podcasts exploring the Flemish cobbled Classics and focusing on a few of the lesser-known races. I would be taking my bike so I could explore the roads of a region that has a slice of bike racing culture lurking around every corner.

'You have to call this the Lionel of Flanders,' he said.

I laughed, because I assumed he was joking.

'I'm being serious,' he said.

'I'm not sure I want to give any impression that I think of myself as a good cyclist,' I said.

'Don't worry,' he said, 'I don't think there's any danger of that.'

And so the Lionel of Flanders was born. Over five days, and accompanied by photographer Simon Gill, I took in three races – Dwars Door Vlaanderen, the E3 Harelbeke and Ghent–Wevelgem – and rode to Roubaix. All three races suit the same sort of rider – the specialists who can cope with cobblestones and crosswinds and have the punch and power to conquer the short, sharp hills – and yet they each have a distinctive character of their own. Ghent–Wevelgem is the oldest, first held in 1934. In the past, it used to hug the coast, where the wind caused havoc, but now it is becoming the race of the battlefields, taking the riders almost cross-country en route to the Kemmelberg climb. Dwars Door Vlaanderen has morphed and evolved over the years and perhaps favours the sprinters more than the other two, and the GP E3 Harelbeke is the baby of the three, dating back to only 1958, and these days enjoying a reputation as the perfect warm-up for the Tour of Flanders. Here is a potted guide to what I learned.

A is for André-Pétrieux

The 500-metre concrete track at the velodrome André-Pétrieux has hosted the finish of Paris–Roubaix since 1943 (except from 1986 to 1988). It is named after a father and his son. André Sr owned a bar nearby and was one of the founders of the Velo Club Roubaix. André Jr was a sports administrator in the town. It's open to the public most of the time so if you choose to ride to Roubaix you'd be very unlucky not to be able to gain access to do a couple of laps. But Roubaix is in France, not Flanders, I hear you say. Actually, it's in the French bit of Flanders, which spills across the border.

B is for Bootel Ahoi

We stayed in Kortrijk, because it was ideally situated for the three races we wanted to see, on a floating hotel called the Bootel Ahoi. It may have lacked space but it was well appointed and served a very good breakfast. Being woken in the morning by the boat's gentle rocking motion is far more pleasant than the harsh trill of a phone's alarm.

C is for cobbles

Or *kasseien*, as they are known in Flemish. You can't take a bike to Flanders and not have a go on the cobbles. The best way to sample them is to head to the Ronde Van Vlaanderen museum in Oudenaarde and pick up a map. From there, the Oude Kwaremont, Paterberg and Koppenberg are three of the most famous cobbled climbs and all are within easy reach.

B is for Bootel Ahoi

D is for Dwars Door Vlaanderen

It loosely translates as 'across Flanders' and in the old days the race crossed from one side of the region to the other. Nowadays it starts in Roeselare and finishes in Waregem. It will do so again in 2018 but the course will be quite different. A date change means the race will take place on the Wednesday before the Tour of Flanders. The plan is there will be only asphalt or concrete climbs – no cobbled hills – and the smooth Knokteberg (also known as the Côte de Trieu) will assume strategic importance.

E is for E3

Only in Belgium could a major bike race be named after a motorway that has long since changed its name. The race, which is thought of as a little

Tour of Flanders, was founded to celebrate the transcontinental network of motorways stretching from Scandinavia to Portugal (the Belgian stretch of which was the E03). The motorway from Antwerp to Kortrijk is now called the E17 but the race remains the E3 Harelbeke.

F is for flags

There are two Flandrian flags featuring the distinctive black lion on a bright yellow background. On the region's official flag the lion has red claws and a tongue. Flandrian separatists, who want to split from the Walloons, wave a flag with an all-black lion. Or is it the other way round? No, I was definitely right the first time.

G is for Gilbert and Greg

Following Tom Boonen's retirement, former teammates Philippe Gilbert and Greg Van Avermaet have developed a very keen rivalry on the cobbles. In 2017, Van Avermaet (a Flandrian) got the upper hand, winning E3 Harelbeke, Ghent–Wevelgem and Paris–Roubaix, although Gilbert (a Walloon) landed a blow of his own, winning the Tour of Flanders.

H is for hangover

There are so many Belgian beers, with different recipes, styles and brewing techniques, producing a range of flavours and each coming in their own attractive bottles and glasses, that the temptation is to try a lot of them. Some of them are fiendishly strong, too, so be wary of bar staff who lull you into a false sense of security by saying something like, 'Oh it's only nine per cent, so quite light really.' It's always the last one that gives you cause for regret.

I is for Iron Briek

They make them hard in Flanders and one of the toughest was Briek Schotte, who earned the nickname Izjeren Briek, or Iron Briek. He won the Tour of Flanders in 1942 and 1948 and a couple of world titles for good measure before going on to run the legendary Flandria team. When he died in 2004, Eddy Merckx, Rik Van Looy, Roger De Vlaeminck, Sean Kelly, Freddy Maertens and Frank Vandenbroucke were among the pallbearers. The Flemish ministry of culture put up an impressive statue of him in his home town, Kanegem, near Tielt, although it's made of bronze, not iron.

J is for Jean-Pierre Monseré

A prodigious talent who won the 1970 world road race in Leicester aged just twenty-two and was killed the following March when he collided with a car during a race near Antwerp. His medals and jerseys are on display in the Wielermuseum (currently in its temporary home in a church while the museum is renovated) in his home town Roeselare, where there's also a cycle route that bears his name. Follow the signs with the rainbow bands on.

K is for Kemmelberg

The Kemmelberg is a charming climb nestled in the woods. It's one of the defining features of Ghent–Wevelgem. My favourite side has big fat cobbles like well-risen loaves and an aesthetically pleasing bend that takes in the contour of the hillside before a steep, straight run to the top. The 'other' side is steep and dead straight, which makes it harder to ride. There are a couple of restaurants on the hill and as a vantage point on race day it's hard to beat.

J is for Jean-Pierre Monseré

L is for Lippenhovestraat

If it's 'flat' stretches of cobbles you're looking for, they don't come much more intimidating than the 1,300-metre section called Lippenhovestraat near Zottegem. It's not far from the equally famous Paddestraat. Both sections feature in many of the cobbled Classics, approached from one direction or other.

M is for moules-frites

A big bowl of fat mussels steamed in white wine and cream and served with a bowl of chips and mayonnaise makes for a perfect lunch.

N is for night life

If you stay in Kortrijk, check out De Dingen, a quirky bar in Budastraat close to the Grote Markt. The place has a vintage furniture shop vibe and one of its regulars is a cat who lives on the premises and mingles with the customers, hopping up on the bar when thirsty, knowing the staff will provide a saucer of water.

N is for night life

O is for Orval

My favourite Belgian beer, although perhaps a controversial choice because it's not from Flanders. This rich, deep-brown Trappist brew is from a town in the Ardennes, very close to the border with France. It's apparently only sporadically available. According to some bar staff I've spoken to, only a certain amount is produced and distributed each month and when it's gone, it's gone.

P is for Plugstreets

In 2017, Ghent–Wevelgem's course took the riders into the battlefields via the Plugstreets – unpaved farm tracks covered in gravel. One of the longer sections took the race past the field where the Christmas Day truce football match between British and German soldiers took place in 1914. Simon and I rode a few sections the day before the race and tagged along with some of the riders who were doing the Ghent–Wevelgem sportive.

P is for Plugstreets

Q is for Quick-Step

Wandering into the Centrum Ronde Van Vlaanderen's café in Oudenaarde wearing a Quick-Step jersey is a bit like turning up for five-a-side football wearing a shirt with 'Messi 10' on the back. Wearing replica jerseys doesn't seem to be the done thing in Belgium, although they cut you some slack if you're foreign. I once wore my 1986 KAS jersey for a ride and when we stopped for coffee the waiter called me 'Kelly' repeatedly. Rarely has there been a less-deserved nickname.

R is for Ronde

To the locals, it's simply De Ronde. The atmosphere on Tour of Flanders day is unlike any other race. Everyone pays attention, even if they're not really into cycling. If you're ever near Oudenaarde, visit the Centrum Ronde Van Vlaanderen to immerse yourself fully in the history and culture of the race. Then have lunch in the café next door and spend a few minutes admiring all the old jerseys on the wall.

S is for showers

They are not open to the public but on our visit to the Roubaix velodrome I managed to persuade someone to unlock the door and let me take a look round the famous stone showers. Each of the simple cubicles has a small plaque bearing the name of a Paris–Roubaix champion.

T is for Tommeke

Tom Boonen retired at the end of the 2017 Paris–Roubaix having finished 13th in his final race. With four victories to his name he holds the record

S is for showers

for most wins on the *pavé* with Roger De Vlaeminck, who was so good in the 1970s he earned the nickname Monsieur Paris–Roubaix. Boonen is affectionately known as Tommeke, which isn't quite as charming a nickname, but it's better than Tornado Tom. As his long-time team boss Patrick Lefevere said, 'He's the perfect son, brother, brother-in-law, lover, or whatever you want . . . '

U is for under-the-table payments

I should add 'allegedly' here. Roger De Vlaeminck and Freddy Maertens were away together for the best part of 70 kilometres in the 1977 Tour of Flanders. The pair were seen arguing when De Vlaeminck refused to work, leaving Maertens to ride on the front most of the way. As a result, De Vlaeminck won the sprint easily but was booed by fans on the podium for sitting on. In the fallout, Maertens alleged De Vlaeminck had offered him money to keep riding (which De Vlaeminck has always denied). Later still, Maertens was stripped of his second place after testing positive for amphetamines. Maertens, who these days can be found working in the Centrum Ronde Van Vlaanderen in Oudenaarde (see the entry for 'R'), never won the Tour of Flanders and still considers himself the moral winner of the 1977 race.

V is for VDB

On our way to the Plugstreets, we stopped for coffee in Ploegsteert. During the First World War, the British soldiers called the village Plugstreet (which would have earned a caution from the Pronunciation Police, no doubt). Ploegsteert is where Frank Vandenbroucke, the troubled genius of Belgian cycling in the late 1990s and early 2000s, grew up. Outrageous performances, doping, a failed suicide attempt and an untimely death from a pulmonary embolism in 2009 aged just thirty-four barely begins to tell the story of VDB. We popped into the Café de la Grand Place where there are pictures of him, his Belgian national team jersey and his bronze medal from the 1992 junior World Championships on the wall.

W is for Waterzooi

A rich, creamy stew originating in Ghent that is traditionally made with fish but is much more commonly found with chicken these days. It goes very well with frites and beer, as most Belgian cuisine does. If that doesn't appeal, try stoverij, the rich Flemish beef stew made with beer.

X marks the spot

A slight cheat this one. Simon and I headed from Kortrijk to Roubaix and as we crossed the border I happened to turn my head to the right to check out the name of the street we were riding along. It was the rue du Dronckaert where one of the most notorious events in modern cycling history happened. Shortly before the 1998 Tour de France was due to start in Dublin, the Festina team soigneur Willy Voet was stopped by customs officers as he crossed the border and a search of his car revealed a boot packed with performance-enhancing drugs.

Y is for Yves Lampaert

Local knowledge goes a long way when it comes to racing in Flanders. Being familiar with the roads, the climbs, the cobbles and particularly the prevailing wind conditions can be the difference between victory and defeat. Quick-Step's Yves Lampaert, who won Dwars Door Vlaanderen, was born in Izegem which is between Roeselare and Waregem where the race starts and finishes. He's also interested in tractors, which is about as Flandrian as it gets.

X marks the spot

Z is for Zulte-Waregem

Z is for Zulte-Waregem

Dwars Door Vlaanderen finishes just outside the Regenboogstadion football ground in Waregem. It's the home of Zulte-Waregem, who qualified for the Europa League in 2017. Regenboogstadion means 'rainbow stadium' and it is so-called because it opened in 1957, the same year Waregem hosted the UCI World Championship road race. That year Rik Van Steenbergen won the last of his three rainbow jerseys, which remained a joint-record, until Peter Sagan won his fourth.

3. GIRO D'ITALIA DIARY: WEEK 1

Daniel Friebe

Thursday, 4 May

Arrival and team presentation, Alghero, Sardinia

Today Fabio Aru and I have more in common than just the hapless loo-brush barnet: Sardinia's prodigal son, the man for whom this *Grande Partenza* seemed customised and home-brewed, is on my budget airline flight from Turin to Alghero. Of course, Aru should be and would be one of the favourites to win this Giro, but a tyre blow-out and knee blow-up at a Sierra Nevada training camp a few weeks ago have forced him to withdraw.

Aru and I are on nodding, awkward-smiling, '*Ciao, come va?*' kind of terms, not much more. I've interviewed him dozens of times over the last three or four years, but never got far beyond the civil but monosyllabic doorman to his inner soul. Even our good friend Ciro Scognamiglio from *La Gazzetta dello Sport*, who can break ice like a pneumatic pickaxe, admits that he finds Aru hard to crack. Astana's head *directeur sportif*, Beppe Martinelli, has told me more or less the same of his star rider.

And so when our eyes meet, Fabio and I nod, both do the excruciating, mouth-closed grimace, dutifully complete our embarrassed '*come va?*' ritual, and both go back to our iPhones.

Fortunately, any fears that the absence of Sardinia's '*bimbo d'oro*' will take the shine off things are allayed as soon as we step off the plane. With its flags and posters and, yes, even bunting, Alghero airport is pinker than a flamingo sex shop. Next comes the taxi-driver test, and as well as the obligatory, time-honoured 'I used to watch it when Pantani was around', there's also the obligatory, time-honoured moan about traffic and why the town council doesn't build new roundabouts for the other 364 days of the year.

Sardinia is ready for the Giro, and the Giro for it.

Friday, 5 May

Stage 1: Alghero–Olbia, 206km
Stage winner: Lukas Pöstlberger
Pink jersey: Lukas Pöstlberger

At about the moment last night when Pippo Pozzato was checking his Instagram or Twitter or Facebook one final time before he and his Wilier Triestina teammates were called on to the stage overlooking Alghero's marina, I was vaguely aware of the Giro director, Mauro Vegni, also frantically tapping away on his touchscreen a few metres away. An hour or so later I found out why: Vegni had just been notified that two of the Bardiani CSF riders, Stefano Pirazzi and Nicola Ruffoni, had tested positive for a banned hormone just a couple of moments before it was their Bardiani team's turn to parade across the stage.

Of course, at the start in Alghero today Ruffoni and Pirazzi were nowhere to be seen. The Bardiani manager, Bruno Reverberi, told us the 'cretins' had already gone home. 'Zio' or 'Uncle' Reverberi is one of those guilty pleasures of covering professional cycling in Italy. Now aged seventy-one, 'Lo Zio' has been managing teams for over half of those years, a living, blustering monument to a bygone and not necessarily more innocent age. In the winter he was put on trial in an investigation into whether riders had been paying for the privilege of riding for second-tier Italian teams. Reverberi contributed one of the more memorable – and the least politically correct – soundbites of the hearings with his retort to one salty line of questioning: 'Nippo-Fantini has got Japanese who are much worse than our riders!'

Reverberi also has only the most porous of filters in his dealings with the press – a trait as appealing to us at it can be exasperating to Bardiani's press officer, Paolo Barbieri, who stands within earshot, trying his best not to wince as his boss barks a potted and pockmarked history of anti-doping in his team. 'Listen, Sella's haematocrit was forty-eight in 2008!' It's maybe too much information, certainly for Barbieri, who manages to stay calmly on message in a huddle of English-speaking reporters a few steps from his manager's soapbox.

The crowds in Alghero are at least large and enthusiastic. The buffet at the finish in Olbia is also sublime – a sprawling banquet of local *piatti tipici* not to mention *vini locali* on a rooftop terrace overlooking the Med. Lionel is doubly thrilled because Lukas Pöstlberger, the surprise winner of today's stage and the first *maglia rosa* of the Giro, was the first rider out of his pack of Panini stickers this morning. Napalm declares he will celebrate tonight with a slap-up meal. Another one.

Saturday, 6 May

Stage 2: Olbia–Tortolì, 221km
Stage winner: André Greipel
Pink jersey: André Greipel

If the first revelation of this Giro was Lukas Pöstlberger, and the second that *culurgiones* are to ravioli what Gianfranco Zola was to the attacking midfield position in turn-of-the-millennium football – Sardinian and brilliant – the third comes with the news that the Volta a Catalunya may hold its own 'Big Start' here in the next three years. Today I discovered that, although it's now three centuries since the Spanish War of Succession began the process of Sardinia's 'Italianicisation', a variant of Catalan is still spoken fluently by about a quarter of the population of Alghero and understood by just over 90 per cent. The Algheresi consider their city a Catalan enclave, a 'Little Barcelona'. This has prompted local officials to begin talks with the organisers of the Volta. There is also a precedent: I find out now that the Volta hopped across the Balearic Sea to Alghero for a time-trial on its penultimate day in 1986, and that Sean Kelly was the stage winner.

This afternoon in the press room I ask Carlo Alberto Melis, *L'Unione Sarda*'s man at the Giro, what he makes of the story. 'Nice idea,' he says, 'but somehow I can't see it.'

Carlo Alberto is a little more optimistic about the Giro's lasting impact on the island. Sardinia has produced only a handful of professional cyclists, by far the most successful of whom, Aru, had to 'emigrate' to the mainland to chase his dream. Carlo Alberto says that cycling is thriving in Sardinia among the MAMIL generation – and that hopefully the Giro being here can be a shot in the arm for the sport at a younger, more competitive level. Not literally a shot in the arm, obviously . . . Italian cycling has had enough of those.

Sunday, 7 May

Stage 3: Tortolì–Cagliari, 148km
Stage winner: Fernando Gaviria
Pink jersey: Fernando Gaviria

The early *maglia rosa* in the general classification of our hotels goes emphatically to last night's pied-à-terre, the Hotel Bia Maore in Baunei. We get there by driving back up today's route, doing what was a descent for the peloton in reverse. Baunei is a gorgeous little hamlet perched on the mountainside above Tortolì, with unencumbered views across the water and towards the Italian mainland. The dusk light hits pastel facades in dazzling yellow and pink strobes. The gentle din from the only bar on the main street will be our mood music late into the night.

These are what colleagues who have covered twenty or thirty editions call *'serate da* Giro'. 'Giro evenings'. Near-as-damn-it perfect evenings.

Tomorrow morning I'll run further up the hill and see graffiti that will remain on the tarmac for months, maybe even years if the 'Forza Pantani' scrawls you can still see on roads all over Italy are any gauge. Just a few hundred metres from our hotel, I look down and see a pink 'Scarponi, always in our hearts' and a 'Michele RIP' spool under my running shoes. There will be many more like this over the course of three weeks. My contact with Scarponi, who was hit by a vehicle in his home village and killed on the eve of the Giro, had been sporadic over several years – the odd interview at races here, a phone-call for a quote there. I am much more closely acquainted with his now, sadly, former agent, Raimondo Scimone. Scimone received several dishonourable mentions in the Padova police investigation that ended up costing Scarponi the second ban of his career, this one for consulting the banned doctor Michele Ferrari. Scarponi's first had, of course, come as a result of Operación Puerto. One day at the Giro, through intermittent sobs, Raimando tells me the story of when he and Michele were flying to Spain in 2007 to review the evidence incriminating Scarponi that the Guardia Civil had seized from Dr Eufemiano Fuentes. When they arrived at the check-in, the lady behind the desk held up three fingers, to which Raimondo replied, 'No, just two of us.'

That wasn't what she meant. It was the third of October. Their booking had been for the second.

Michele had burst out laughing – cackled so hard and for so long it left him doubled over in pain – which is why Raimondo is telling the story for me now. 'That was typical of Mickey. It was such a tense situation, one of the worst times of his life, yet as always his sense of humour defused all the stress . . .'

The anecdote also brings levity to an awkward topic of conversation. For many, for much of his career Scarponi was considered a villain, and yet the unsavoury footnotes to his career must also now coexist and be contextualised alongside fond memories of a nice man who brought joy to many lives and will leave a large void.

The show, the Giro, must go on, but it is comforting for friends like Scimone to know that here at the Corsa Rosa – a race Scarponi 'won' in 2010 due to Alberto Contador's own doping ban – he will not be forgotten.

Monday, 8 May

Rest day, Sicily

Our smugness at having booked a cheap Ryanair flight from Sardinia to Sicily months ago, thus sparing us overnight sea-sick-mageddon on a ferry or a six-hour, two-flight odyssey via the mainland, has dissipated within hours of us touching down in Catania. First we try to record the last segment of our stage three episode in the airport car park and are immediately set upon by a plague of mosquito-horsefly chimeras. We then drive two hours to our B&B near Cefalù, fall through the door of the restaurant next door just in time for last orders, but it is and will remain the worst meal of the Giro. I sleep badly, miss my morning run, and we have our first Cycling Podcast team barney of the Giro en route to Team Sky's hotel in Palermo. The blow-up is an HD snapshot of typical traits: Richard being Buffaloey, with every missed turning and lost minute inching Napalm ever closer to a stress explosion . . . and me playing the sulky, impenetrable, wantonly obtuse teenager in the back of the car.

Fortunately, we all come around and it turns into a relatively fruitful rest day. I manage to call Fernando Gaviria 'Francisco' at a Quick-Step press thingy. There are a few nervous moments when a group of middle-aged men whom I imagine to have names like Vito, Rosario and Pasquale seem to very deliberately form a semi-circle around one side of our (white!) Maserati just as we're about to pull away after our lunch stop. The only restaurant near our digs is the same joint as last night, with its laminated menus and deep-fried sea-life that could just as easily have been fished out of a nearby squash court as from the ocean. But, but, I've managed to get out for my run, we're all friends again and, yes, we're still at the Giro. So, breathe . . .

Fernando Gaviria and his pink jersey

Tuesday, 9 May

Stage 4: Cefalù–Etna, 181km
Stage winner: Jan Polanc
Pink jersey: Bob Jungels

The first mountain-stage of the Giro is a stinker – and I'm not talking about the whiff of sulphur swirling around Etna's crater. The issue seems to have been the wind; it can't really be a headwind all the way, as the road swings in mazy zig-zags across the volcano, surely into and then away

Scaling the volcano. The Giro on Etna

with the breeze coming off the sea. The riders, though, are adamant: whenever anyone tried to accelerate they got blown backwards. The only exception clearly was UAE's Jan Polanc, a man with previous as a mountain-stage *guastafeste* or spoilsport, having won on the Abetone two years ago. That was the day when Mario Cipollini stopped a few Acqua di Parma-doused whiskers from accusing Alberto Contador of using a motorised bike or wheel live on TV. It may also have been the day when the erstwhile Lion King said on air it pained him to see Vincenzo Nibali 'in a team with Kazakhs, speaking Kazakh'; or indeed when, on the back of a short but heart-warming feature on the Ethiopian debutant Tsgabu Grmay, we were taken back to the studio and a visibly disconcerted Cipo. 'You know,' he sighed, 'we've given these Africans bikes and if we're not careful they'll be coming over here winning our races . . .'

Yes, among so many guilty pleasures or at least amusements at the Giro, Cipo is maybe the guiltiest. Too guilty, in fact. And no longer much of a pleasure. We learned a few days ago – because every local and national paper reported it – that Cipollini has been accused by his ex-wife of physically assaulting her in a gym in Lucca in January, a few days after they had been officially divorced. Police are investigating whether the most prolific stage winner in Giro history did indeed grab his former partner by the neck and leave her needing first aid, as she claims. Cipo of course denies the allegations.

Lionel, Richard and Daniel recording the podcast in a bar on Mount Etna

Wednesday, 10 May

Stage 5: Pedara–Messina, 159km
Stage winner: Fernando Gaviria
Pink jersey: Bob Jungels

After three days and two stages, I board the ferry taking us from Sicily and to the mainland with pangs of regret. I have lived in Italy twice and visited several times a year for the last two decades. I so shamelessly embrace Italian culture and customs that friends think I've based my life around Kevin Costner's character in *American Flyers*. But this has been my first time in Sicily. Not only has it been a short stay but I feel we've only very lightly skimmed some of the island's least interesting areas. Most Italians swoon at the mere mention of the Siracusa, rave about Ragusa, but the Giro has taken us to only a short sliver of northern coastline and then around Etna's base. We have eaten cannoli, arancini and granite, but not other specialities like pasta alla norma or caponata. I daren't tell Lionel.

I'll also sheepishly admit that the germ of my fascination with Sicily, like a lot of people's, is the mafia. It came not from *The Godfather*, its spin-offs, sequels or imitations, but from one of my old Italian professors, John Dickie, his lectures, and a book he wrote a few years ago about what is in fact only the Sicilian branch of a network of crime syndicates across southern Italy, Cosa Nostra. Thanks to another of Dickie's books, I have become even more intrigued, even more darkly fascinated by Cosa Nostra's younger, now more violent and richer Calabrian equivalent – the 'Ndrangheta. Nowhere else, though, do even mere landscapes, faces and gestures feed and infuse the mafia-linked mythology and paranoia as much as in Sicily. Way back when he was a neo-pro, Vincenzo Nibali of all people assured me it was possible to live and grow up on the island and never remotely experience the influence of the clans. Nonetheless, the very fact that I was asking – and that Nibali told me he had already answered questions on this subject countless times – demonstrated that the mafia's aura and mark on Sicily's history at least, if not its present, remain inescapable.

Today of course marks Nibali's homecoming to Messina. The crowds packed into the city's streets are large and unruly. Unfortunately, the atmosphere in and around Nibali's Bahrain-Merida team bus is rather sombre, even a little dark. The young Slovenian, Luka Pibernik, escaped from the peloton on the penultimate of two city circuits and proceeded to raise his arms in celebration as he crossed the line marking the end of lap one. The gaffe was greeted with widespread amusement – except, apparently, in his team. 'What the hell was he doing?' I overhear Alberto Volpi, one of the *directeurs sportifs*, wonder aloud. Pibernik looks straight at me as I try to intercept him on his way to the team bus . . . then shakes his head and disappears up the steps.

Thursday, 11 May

Stage 6: Reggio Calabria–Terme Luigiane, 217km
Stage winner: Silvan Dillier
Pink jersey: Bob Jungels

Today's stage finish makes history as the worst-smelling that I've ever covered in my seventeen years as a journalist. The sulphurous stench wafting over the finish line from the adjacent Terme Luigiane spa baths has riders snatching towels to cover their noses, or sprinting off, out of their saddles, to the refuge of their team buses. The purported healing properties of the waters and their vapours are surely mitigated by the vague sense of having stumbled upon a giant open-air public toilet.

Fortunately, tonight's surroundings are a lot more salubrious. When I tell an old photographer friend, Pier Maulini, that our hotel is in a place called Civita, he enthusiastically informs me that this is a famous Albanian enclave. I subsequently discover that the town was founded in the fifteenth century by Albanian refugees from the Ottoman invasion. Today, Civita retains its status as a stronghold of the Arbëreshë or Italo-Albanian ethnic minority formally recognised by the Italian state. Moreover, most of the Civitesi still communicate in the Arbëresh language.

Lionel is, of course, most conversant in the vernacular of food – and the travails of a stressful day, with long drives and troublesome recordings, are merrily dispatched with a plate of Arbëresh Dromast – tiny flour dumplings sprinkled with oregano water in a rich tomato sauce. As with most of the best restaurants in Italy, there's no menu – the chef or restaurant owner simply comes to the table and runs through what's on tonight.

Civita, in the heart of the Albanian community founded in Calabria

It's also almost shamefully cheap – €70 for three of us, with wine, every available delicacy and a *digestivo* on the house to finish.

Even with half of tomorrow's KM0 still to record, the mood in the camp is much improved and we fairly bounce up the 25 per cent incline through the old town to our bed and breakfast.

Friday, 12 May

Stage 7: Castrovillari–Alberobello, 224km
Stage winner: Caleb Ewan
Pink jersey: Bob Jungels

Alberobello brings yet another reminder of the degree to which Italian cycling and the Giro are still stalked by their dark recent past and its

Our b&b host brings a bottle of light podcasting wine

protagonists. Having briefed Lionel on the 'trulli' – the white, conical houses with which Alberobello and Puglia's now thriving luxury tourism industry are synonymous – I also explain to him why Leonardo Piepoli was known as the 'trullo volante' or literally the flying 'trullo', namely that he grew up in Alberobello. As far as I'm aware, Piepoli hasn't been seen at a major race since his positive test for CERA at the 2007 Tour de France . . . until today. We've been in the press-room about an hour or so when I look up from my laptop, spy a small circle of Italian colleagues in one of the gangways and Piepoli holding forth in the middle. Surprised and intrigued, I immediately walk over to see and hear what's going on.

Prior to his ban I spoke to Piepoli a few times at races and more recently over the phone, but I'd be shocked if he recognised me. Nevertheless, he isn't in the least bit fazed that I'm now listening in to what is turning into quite a monologue. I was aware that he had started coaching pro riders, but not that one of the golden boys of Italian

cycling, Davide Formolo, was among them. I wonder whether
Cannondale's team manager, Jonathan Vaughters, knows, and, if he does,
what he thinks given the team's staunchly anti-doping image. I'm also, I
must confess, quite impressed that Piepoli is speaking so openly and at
such length, given that he vanished with nary a word after the positive
test in 2007. Most notably, he says that, albeit then from afar, he noticed
a major attitude shift among younger riders when the UCI introduced its
no-needle policy in 2011. When Piepoli was growing up as a cyclist,
syringes filled with legal vitamin solutions acted as a gateway to 'soft
doping' like corticosteroids justified with phoney TUEs, then later to
rocket fuels like EPO; nowadays, he tells us, it's pointless and even
unfair to quiz the likes of Formolo about doping because he and his
peers don't know the first thing about illegal performance enhancement
and also shouldn't bear the burden of their forefathers' guilt.

The issue unfortunately is that talk is relatively cheap even from
Piepoli, certainly when Italian cycling and the Giro remain a sprawling
Madame Tussauds of former dopers and their enablers. A few years ago,
the state broadcaster, RAI, had Danilo Di Luca appearing as a guest on
their post-stage review – while he was serving a doping ban. Barely
anyone in Italy flinched, and there was definitely no mass outcry. We
perhaps then saw one result of such moral ambivalence in 2013, when
Di Luca was doped and caught again and finally banned for life.

Caleb Ewan narrowly takes the stage win, ahead of Fernando
Gaviria. As Ewan celebrates, I hear various riders grumbling to each
other about the precariousness of the finishing circuit, and a group of
teenage girls squealing as they catch a glimpse of *Grey's Anatomy* actor
Patrick Dempsey. Dempsey is here as a guest of BMC and their co-
sponsor Tag Heuer, but is mainly hanging out with Ivan Basso, who
works for Trek–Segafredo.

It's a funny old game.

4. GIRO D'ITALIA DIARY: WEEK 2

Lionel Birnie

Saturday, 13 May

Stage 8: Molfetta–Peschici, 189km
Stage winner: Gorka Izagirre
Pink jersey: Bob Jungels

It's been three days but I am yet to fully recover from the low point of the Giro – the moment I realised a sixteen-minute interview with Tom Dumoulin had failed to record properly because, idiot that I am, I'd plugged the headphones into the microphone jack. Dumoulin had talked engagingly about the Giro and Italy and about holidaying in Umbria last year, not far from Montefalco where the time trial, or wine trial, will take place in a few days' time. Forget it and move on, my brain is telling me, but I keep listening to the recording and hoping by some miracle it will have repaired itself.

On our way to Molfetta, we get trapped in a network of narrow side streets and, not for the first or last time, I have to thread the Maserati between parked cars with barely a hair's breadth for clearance. Even though I say so myself, it was the most impressive piece of driving in a Maserati since Richard's legendary 27-point turn in Catanzaro at the start of the 2016 Giro – a spectacle that brought people out of their houses to offer guidance (or to snigger) and which is still spoken about in hushed tones in bars and cafés to this day.

I head to the Bora-Hansgrohe bus to present Lukas Pöstlberger with the inaugural Pédaleur de Charme award of the new Grand Tour season. When I tell him he was nominated and voted for by our listeners he is genuinely touched.

The approach to Peschici on the Puglia coast is stunning. The road rises and dips through the woods and then we catch sight of the rocky coast and white-walled buildings. The tight corner at the bottom of the final climb almost causes the car to run aground and so it's not such a surprise later on when Valerio Conti of UAE-Team Emirates comes a cropper on the same bend, blowing any chance of securing Italy's first stage victory of this Giro. His miscalculation opens the door for Gorka Izagirre and in the subsequent podcast we wonder why Movistar allowed one of Nairo Quintana's key support riders off the leash the day before such an important stage.

Sunday, 14 May

Stage 9: Montenero di Bisaccia–Blockhaus, 149km
Stage winner: Nairo Quintana
Pink jersey: Nairo Quintana

As we expected, Nairo Quintana wins the stage and takes the pink jersey but when the dust settles and we study the results we see his efforts have not landed the decisive blow he probably hoped for. He puts a minute into Vincenzo Nibali admittedly, but Thibaut Pinot is only 24 seconds back, with Tom Dumoulin for company. It is Dumoulin's performance that changes the complexion of the race because the time trial puts him in pole position in the theoretical general classification, even if the mountains in the final week tilt the pendulum back in Quintana's direction.

Unfortunately, it is a crash that generates the big story of the day. After the descent leading to the bottom of the Blockhaus climb there was a benign stretch of straight road. A police motorcyclist chose that as the safest place to stop but the group of favourites used the full width of the road, as they were entitled to do, and the result was that Wilco Kelderman clipped the motorcycle and he, Geraint Thomas and Mikel Landa of Sky, were among those who crashed.

Thomas loses five minutes, Landa more than twenty-seven, and suddenly Sky's two-pronged assault on the race is reduced to nothing.

Incidents with motorcycles have become all too common in the last couple of years and there have been some tragic outcomes, so in the grand scheme of things this is a fairly minor one, although it has undoubtedly influenced the race.

In these circumstances, it's too easy to become part of a mob calling for Something To Be Done and even easier to blame the motorcyclist saying he shouldn't have stopped where he did. No one wants the result of the race to be decided by an accident caused by an outside influence, but motorcycles are actually an important part of the race. They work in relay to secure stretches of road and their job becomes even harder when the peloton breaks into bits and there are multiple groups to look out for. From the safety of the press room or the sofa we can tell them they're getting it all wrong without ever having to take the risks and decisions they take.

Monday, 15 May

Rest day, Spoleto

In all my years covering the Grand Tours, I have never missed lunch on a rest day until today. I am still not quite sure how it happened. After a leisurely breakfast, Daniel and I sit down to record an episode of *Kilometre 0*. The subject is The Double, and whether a rider could win the Giro d'Italia and Tour de France in the same season.

As Nairo Quintana has just taken the pink jersey it seems logical to wonder whether he has what it takes to become the first rider since

Marco Pantani in 1998 to win both. We chew over the various factors that make it a much more difficult proposition these days and in the end come to the conclusion that The Double (certainly in terms of winning the Giro and Tour) will not be done this season.

By the time we've recorded the episode and sent it to our producer to polish and tighten, it's lunch time. Our bed and breakfast on the outskirts of Spoleto doesn't offer lunch, so I decide to head to town to find a launderette and somewhere to eat. I have success on one front but not the other and as I load Daniel's pants and T-shirts into one machine and mine into another, hunger causes my stomach to do a passable impression of a washing machine by gurgling loudly.

Lionel on launderette duty in Spoleto

Once the laundry is dried and folded I head back to the hotel and then Simon, Daniel and I drive to a gelateria on the outskirts of town. We need a picture to illustrate The Double episode and Daniel has come up with the idea of photographing two scoops of ice cream – one pink, one yellow to represent the *maglia rosa* and *maillot jaune*.

Pink and yellow ice cream for the maglia rosa and maillot jaune

I learn about Italian gelateria etiquette. If a customer orders chocolate and vanilla, he or she would expect to see the chocolate served first with the vanilla on top, not the other way round.

Just as my stomach is greeting the first drops of strawberry ice cream and wondering if this is all there's going to be for lunch I manage to drop my ice cream on the floor. I watch it fall in slow motion and splatter at my feet. As metaphors for cycling's increasingly elusive Double go, this seems apposite. Finally, I have to drive to Foligno to meet former professional Dan Lloyd for a quick interview in the Maserati. As I ask him about the highs and lows of riding the Giro I realise I've driven into a very narrow dead-end. Dan comes to the rescue and, showing impressive spatial awareness and the sort of full-lock-to-full-lock steering wheel technique a fork lift truck driver would be proud of, gets us out of a tight spot.

When I finally get something to eat, in the delightful Il Tempio del Gusto in Spoleto, I munch through half a dozen breadsticks like a cartoon alligator demolishing a wooden jetty.

Tuesday, 16 May

Stage 10: Foligno–Montefalco, 39.8km
Stage winner: Tom Dumoulin
Pink jersey: Tom Dumoulin

Back in Sardinia, I had set myself the task of completing the Giro 100 Panini sticker album, released to celebrate the great anniversary of the race, but I now realise this is not going to happen.

As we recorded the podcast in Olbia on the opening day of the race, I opened my first packet and the very first sticker to come out was Lukas Pöstlberger, who not two hours earlier had won the stage. It felt like the stickers possessed the powers of a sort of reverse Nostradamus but any belief that I could predict the stage winners of the Giro by investing the stickers with the soothsaying quality of tarot cards was dashed more or less immediately because Filippo Pozzato was next out.

Since then the stickers had been hard to come by. I managed to get some in Cefalù in Sicily, and some more in Reggio Calabria, but it was very disappointing to find they weren't being sold in service stations. It meant that whenever I found the stickers on sale in a tobacconist or sweet shop I would swap a ten- or twenty-euro note for as many packets as that bought me. I'd then open them in secret so Richard and Daniel didn't know what podcast funds were being squandered on.

Collecting the stickers was like regressive therapy, taking me back to my childhood when the peculiar currency of the playground was Football '84 Panini stickers and a messed-up economy that meant six Ian Rushes (world-class striker) were worth one Frankie Bunn (inexplicably rare and rubbish Luton Town player).

So far I've spent a fortune, I've still got hundreds of gaps in the album and my brick-sized pile of swapsies contains six Sergey Firsanovs (Gazprom). I had no idea these collections were so expensive to complete but to see this job through is going to cost hundreds of euros.

Last year, we visited the Maserati factory in Modena and were shown the multi-storey car park that contained the sports car collection of the Panini company's founder. Now I understood how he could afford such a collection.

Tom Dumoulin crushes everyone to win the wine trial, held in the beautiful vineyards around Montefalco. Only three riders got within two minutes of the Dutchman's time as he took the pink jersey and gave himself a lead of more than two-and-a-half minutes over Nairo Quintana. At the other end of the field, poor Matteo Pelucchi, who crashed hard on the stage to Etna and had been bandaged up like a mummy since, finished more than sixteen minutes down, outside the time limit. I sift through my Panini stickers. The Giro has no Matteo Pelucchis, but I've got two.

Wednesday, 17 May

Stage 11: Florence–Bagno di Romagna, 161km
Stage winner: Omar Fraile
Pink jersey: Tom Dumoulin

Daniel heads off to Florence to meet Mark Cavendish and the Moto GP rider Cal Crutchlow and Simon and I skip the start and head straight to Balze, a village not far from the top of the Monte Fumaiolo climb.

We find a restaurant and ask for a table. All that's on offer is the fixed lunch menu, which turns out to be a large slice of lasagne, followed by a plate of salad, then some sage butter ravioli, then braised rabbit and finally a piece of tiramisu. By the time I've finished that lot I feel like Henry the Eighth.

At some point, a couple of British cycling fans are seated at the table next to ours. It turns out they're on holiday nearby and he had persuaded his partner to make a day-trip to the Giro. I get the feeling he'd had to give the Giro a pretty big sell. 'We've been listening to the podcast in the car,' he says. 'I've actually started to enjoy it,' she says.

When we finish eating, Simon offers to give our new friends a lift to the top of the climb and they leave me to waddle up the hill to find a café showing the race on television.

I spend a very enjoyable afternoon watching one of the most intriguing tactical battles of the Giro so far as Omar Fraile outfoxes Rui Costa, Pierre Rolland and Tanel Kangert at the finish.

When the race is over and the crowds begin to make their way down the hill, I find a bit of shady grass and lie down to let lunch settle while waiting for Simon to return.

Thursday, 18 May

Stage 12: Forlì–Reggio Emilia, 229km
Stage winner: Fernando Gaviria
Pink jersey: Tom Dumoulin

Forlì has a large, attractive arcaded square. I think it's probably my favourite large, attractive arcaded square of the Giro yet, so I pull up a chair outside a café and order a coffee.

I spot Bahrain-Merida's mascot, Falco the falcon, a man (I presume) in a cartoonish bird costume, standing around waving at children. I'm perhaps reading too much into the poor bird's body language here but he (or she) has the slumped shoulders so often seen among the poor convicts of the publicity caravan by this stage of the race. I suspect Falco is finding out just what a test of endurance the Grand Tours can be. There was going to be a joke in here about the occupant of the suit observing some kind of punishment but the Bahrain regime has such a terrible sense of humour about these things that I'll direct you to the country's Amnesty International report instead.

I take a sip of my caramel mochaccino topped with whipped cream (just kidding, Daniel) and muse that all the teams in the World Tour should have a mascot.

Of course, Sky's mascot would be a robot with a range of pithy phrases to help motivate the riders.

'Great. Cycling. G,' it would say in a metallic tone.

'Watts – high.'

'Margins gained – four.'

In the afternoon, we arrive in Reggio Emilia, which sits in a sweetspot of northern Italy that seems to be home to just about everything that's great about the country. Reggio Emilia is where Parmigiano Reggiano cheese comes from. Just up the road is Parma, famous for the ham, and the same distance in the other direction is Modena, home of balsamic vinegar, Maserati cars and Panini stickers. On our way into town we pass the Mapei Stadium, where Serie A team Sassuolo play. The club is the latest passion of Giorgio Squinzi, whose previous plaything was the formidable Mapei cycling team that straddled the turning of the millennium like a colossus.

Delicious parma ham

The buffet laid on for the press is fabulous. There's a huge wheel of Parmigiano Reggiano to hack at, slices of delicious moist ham and a glass of fizzy red Lambrusco, a wine that has a terrible reputation in Britain because everyone associates it with being cheap and unpleasant. The red is a revelation and I later discover that the local producers can't give the stuff away to the British, which puzzles them seeing as we guzzle so much prosecco.

I think back to last year's Giro, when we stayed up in the Friuli region. Our hotel owner was all linen trousers and moccasins, bouffant hair and a self-satisfied tan, and although I couldn't understand what he was saying, Daniel explained the gist, which was that he thanked all the Brits for buying up every drop of his prosecco, even the stuff he wouldn't wash his sports car with, so that he could afford to buy another chunk of the village.

The stage is won by Fernando Gaviria. It's his third victory of the

The Maserati at the Verdanoce Agriturismo

race, which is his debut Grand Tour, remember, and as he struts into the press room he has the air of a young man who has just sold a vast quantity of really terrible prosecco to a British importer for an inflated price and knows he has much more where that came from.

Our hotel is absolutely stunning, with a long vine-flanked gravel drive leading up to a beautiful villa. It's so good, I'll give it a name check – it's the Verdanoce Agriturismo, a short drive south of Reggio Emilia. If you go, tell them *The Cycling Podcast* says hello. I doubt they'll remember so just mention we were the two clowns in the white Maserati. Dinner is equally impressive – a delicate ravioli, followed by a spatchcocked pigeon and then strawberries in balsamic vinegar.

Friday, 19 May

Stage 13: Reggio Emilia–Tortona, 167km
Stage winner: Fernando Gaviria
Pink jersey: Tom Dumoulin

Dave Brailsford is putting on his y'know brave face in the light of Geraint Thomas's woes. The Welshman has had to concede defeat following the crash on the road to Blockhaus. An astonishing second place to Dumoulin in the wine trial had masked his injuries for only so long and, as Brailsford says, you don't take chances with knee injuries, so it's time to go home and recover for the Tour.

We reach Tortona in good time, so I head from the press room to the centre of town to find the shops in the main arcade have been transformed into a Fausto Coppi museum. Coppi died here in the town's hospital in January 1960 aged forty. It's one of those stories of intrigue and conspiracy the Italians seem to specialise in. He'd been on a trip to Burkina Faso (then Upper Volta) with Jacques Anquetil, Louison Bobet and Raphaël Géminiani, among others. He fell ill, as did Géminiani, who was diagnosed with malaria. Coppi's doctors dismissed malaria as a possibility and he died. Years later, a monk who had been in Burkina Faso said Coppi was poisoned. The claim was dismissed by those who treated him as nonsense. In 2002, an investigation was opened and there were plans to exhume his body but the case was closed again before that happened. Nevertheless it all adds to the Coppi legend.

Tortona's streets have the grace and style of late 1950s Italy, or maybe it's the ever-present air of Fausto Coppi that's giving it that impression. The shop windows are decorated with the usual Giro celebratory stuff, pink balloons and bunting, but also with photographs of Fausto (and his brother Serse, who often gets overlooked). One shop has a magnificent Bianchi bike that looks like it's been wrapped in blankets and kept in storage for half a century it's so pristine. Another has a framed photograph of the local paper's front page announcing Coppi's death, its edges printed black in mourning and respect. Then, out of nowhere, there's a Mapei jersey with its brightly coloured cubes, which seems a little out of place.

We watch the sprint finish from the press tent positioned, as usual, a few hundred metres past the finish and have a fantastic view of the peloton coming over the hill and rushing almost kamikaze style downhill to the line. Gaviria wins for the second day in a row and has the points jersey in the bag providing he can get over the mountains and reach Milan.

Saturday, 20 May

Stage 14: Castellania–Santuario di Oropa, 131km
Stage winner: Tom Dumoulin
Pink jersey: Tom Dumoulin

We're on our way to Castellania, the tiny village where the great Fausto Coppi grew up. We drive through the hills in silence until Daniel says exactly what I was thinking.

'It's strange to realise that Fausto Coppi saw all this in colour too.'

I know exactly what he means. Coppi is such an icon of the black-and-white age that it's difficult to get your head around the fact that he saw the world in vivid, bright colours. He's synonymous with the Bianchi brand and yet it's hard to picture him in their iconic blue jersey because we think of him in shades of grey.

As we reach the village a marshal in a fluorescent vest tells us we can go no further. We're hours early so there's plenty of time to get a coffee before walking up the hill to the team buses.

Looking on the map it can only be a kilometre and a half, two at a push, to the stretch of road where the team buses are due to park up. Daniel could run that in about five or six minutes. We walk briskly and stop where we think the buses will arrive. Then we wait. And wait.

I watch as cyclists pedal past us, marvelling at how old-school Italian club cycling still is. A lot of the riders wear multi-coloured club jerseys plastered in logos for local building firms. There are a lot of beautiful old bikes on show too, the pick of the bunch being a bright red Colnago with chrome forks and rear stays that must date back to the late 1970s or early 1980s.

There comes a point when we realise the buses aren't going to arrive. We double-check the map in the roadbook and we're definitely in the right place so something must have changed. We march to the top of the hill to see what's going on. Another marshal tells us the buses are parking somewhere else. There's been a change of plan, evidently. Daniel makes a call to the Giro press office. The buses are parking at an unspecified location that's not the one marked in the roadbook. The change of plan was made at some point in the recent past but had not been communicated to the media working on the race, it seems.

We start to walk back down the hill. Daniel starts running, quickly dropping me, clearly unaware that in a two-up time trial the time is taken when the second rider crosses the line. I could run, I think. I'm not running, I decide. I settle for a fast walk.

At some point Daniel realises he's also dropped Gianni Savio, his much-loved microphone cover that resembles the silver-haired fox of Italian cycling. 'Did you see Gianni Savio?' he says.

'No, where?' I reply, thinking he means the real Gianni Savio.

Sunday, 21 May

Stage 15: Valdengo–Bergamo, 199km
Stage winner: Bob Jungels
Pink jersey: Tom Dumoulin

I chat to Cannondale-Drapac sports director Charly Wegelius at the start. Charly is looking forward to the mountain stages. 'For me, the Stelvio and the whole Bormio-Livigno region is pretty meaningful, not just because of the races but because I spent a lot of time training there,' he says. 'When I used to ride the Giro and then the Vuelta, I'd spend most of July in Livigno and spend a lot of time on the Stelvio with Aldo Sassi [his coach].

'In 2005 we did a stage of the Giro that went over the Stelvio and finished in Livigno. I was right in the midst of it until about two kilometres from the top before you drop down to Livigno. I absolutely went to pieces and just stopped in the road. At most I was doing about three or four kilometres an hour all the way to the top.

'Fortunately, our hotel was right next to the finish line in Livigno. My masseur pushed me up the stairs one step at a time and I fell asleep on my bed with my kit on, helmet on, radio earpiece in, shoes on, gloves on. So, yeah, I went pretty deep that day, but time heals all doesn't it? Sometimes I'm following in the car, watching the riders, thinking, "How on earth did I manage to do this?" It's pretty amazing what the riders do.'

When we reach Bergamo, we follow a hand-written sign to the car park for press and officials. Daniel just about manages to get the Maserati down the ramp only to find a queue of cars. The car park is full and now he has to reverse back up the ramp, tyres squeaking against the high kerb on both sides. We park in a side street and I spend the afternoon going back and forwards feeding the meter because it will only accept three-euro payments at a time. On one of these trips, a bike in a furniture shop window catches my eye. It's another Bianchi, but this time from 1987. It's Moreno Argentin's time trial bike from an age when these machines looked so futuristic. It's white with the rainbow jersey bands on the frame and forks, it has a flamboyantly curved top tube, cow horn-style handlebars and two white disc wheels made by Campagnolo. I bet it's an absolute dog to ride, like trying to play golf with a mashie niblick now.

Bob Jungels wins the stage with a devastating finish and it feels strange to think it was only a week ago we were wondering whether he would be the talented all-rounder to thwart the likes of Quintana and Nibali. Now that man looks like being Dumoulin, especially after his brilliant win at Oropa yesterday.

After recording the podcast, we head for a pizza with Manolo from the Giro's press office and all our English-speaking colleagues from the press room. It's a shame not to be able to try the polenta so I make a note to return to Bergamo for Il Lombardia one day soon.

5. A LOVE LETTER TO THE PEACOCK OF SANDRIGO

Ciro Scognamiglio

Pippo Pozzato

'If I wasn't so good-looking, you'd never have heard of Fabian Cancellara.'

Does this quote ring any bells? It may well do, albeit with a slight twist. The name at the end of the original version was the footballer Pelé, not Cancellara, and the statement came originally from George Best. Now the guy talking is Filippo Pozzato. He said these words and certainly believed them. Pozzato the professional cyclist, but much more than that. Pozzato the man, but more than that, too. A soul sister – to be precise, my soul sister. Yep, that's it. That's what Filippo Pozzato is. He's unique. There's no one else like him. More than that, we can say that there'll never be anyone like him. I'm absolutely certain of that.

Filippo Pozzato and Fabian Cancellara were teammates in Mapei's 'nursery team' at the start of the noughties and linked up again as fully fledged pros at Fassa Bortolo. They were both strong riders, very strong riders. Maybe Pippo was slightly stronger. But now that Cancellara's hung up his bike the comparison looks rather redundant. 'Spartacus' retired with seven Monuments to his name: a San Remo, three Flanders, three Roubaix. Pozzato is still dining out on his one San Remo. Cancellara can point to his four world time-trial titles and Olympic gold medal. Pozzato's got . . . great hair. We could go on. But that's not the point. Pozzato is unique for who he is. For how he is. For everything he represents. Because even trying to imitate him would be a futile exercise.

Could he have won more? Absolutely. We also can't ignore what he has achieved: that glorious San Remo victory, a stage of the Giro, stages in the Tour, an Italian national champion's jersey, a Tirreno–Adriatico, Het Volk, Hamburg, Plouay. Second places at San Remo, Roubaix and Flanders. A fourth place in a World Championship road race that he 'threw down the toilet', as he says of the 2010 edition won by Thor Hushovd in Geelong. 'I didn't think I'd ride so well. I didn't feel that great, and so I launched my sprint from a long way out. But the others must have been even more tired than me. If only I'd come out of their wheels . . . '

Not having come home from Australia with a medal still grates, seven years on. Fortunately, Pozzato doesn't take himself too seriously – or perhaps even seriously enough. While other riders excel in sprinting or climbing, Filippo shines in self-mockery. Bear in mind that he has one photo of himself in action on the wall at home, and it's not of him winning; Pozzato's arms are aloft, the Colosseum provides the magnificent backdrop . . . and our favourite gladiator is under the mistaken impression that he is the winner of the 2013 Roma Maxima, having failed to realise that a solo escapee, Blel Kadri of AG2R, has already crossed the line. 'Without radios it's an absolute shambles . . . I've made myself look a right prat,' our hero said when a reporter broke the bad news. Now the picture that hangs in his bedroom serves as a reminder to never take himself too seriously.

How or why did Filippo Pozzato become my soul sister? I honestly can't explain . . . and so I asked him. 'We're total opposites. First of all, I actually like working, whereas you're bone idle,' was his reply. He's not totally wrong – in fact he's quite right – but it's more than that. I can confirm that he does take his job seriously, but also that he enjoys the finer things in life. The combination may not be a recipe for success – but it's not necessarily a contradiction, either. Filippo is honest, above all. Never hypocritical. And generous. I suppose that's what I like about him. He's probably only got one year of his pro career left, after which he'll probably, hopefully carry on working in cycling. 'I had three dreams,' he says. 'One was winning Milan–San Remo, which I've achieved. Another was getting a rainbow jersey, which won't happen now. And the third is . . . becoming a father. Who knows?'

You see, Filippo is a man of hidden depths. Take comments like this, for example: 'I always say to fellow riders that cycling is an incredibly intense parenthesis in our lifetimes, but remember that there's more to life. Try to squeeze as much out of these years as possible and learn as much as possible, because cycling is a university of life.'

He can also be passionate and outspoken, particularly on the issue of how cycling nurtures and cares for its young. 'It's an absolute disgrace that there are kids in junior categories already living like professionals. As a kid you have to enjoy yourself and develop without any pressure, otherwise you'll never be able to last a whole career, or even have margins for improvement when the time does come to make it your job. It's unacceptable that there are juniors who are skin and bone and training in November and December, when we professionals are resting. At that age cycling should be a game. When I say these things people tell me that times have changed, but I think we need to wake up because grinding kids into the ground is not the way to go. You should only start learning how to be a rider as an under-23. Then, once you've turned pro, teams should give you time to grow. Instead, riders get dumped as soon as they have a setback. They're not given room to express themselves, no one sympathises if they have personal problems, and no one waits for them if they have physical problems that need fixing. I know it's a complex debate but at the moment so many talents are getting wasted. Unless we start paying attention and investing resources, it's only going to get worse for future generations. I'm not disputing that a champion has to stand out from the rest, but over the years I've learned that athletes are very fragile people and we need to acknowledge that.'

Is this not a fantastic message? So what if the Peacock of Sandrigo, his home town in the Veneto region, seldom spreads his wings nowadays, and hasn't won a race since 2013? I actually prefer it that way, and was terrified the spell would be broken when Filippo was momentarily in danger of winning a stage of the 2016 Giro. Fortunately, that day the German Roger Kluge managed to pip him on the line. I almost scolded him as he arrived back at his team bus that afternoon. 'Were you trying to ruin everything?'

Ciro and his notebook. A permanent reminder of his Soul Sister

Filippo's dream now is to build his own team once he's retired from racing. A team with a new, innovative, successful vision of cycling. Once he told me: 'I want it to be the Real Madrid of cycling.' I didn't reply, but I thought, 'Who cares if it's the Real Madrid, the Anderlecht or the Omonia Nicosia from Cyprus? All that matters is that it's yours, dear Filippo. My soul sister. Until the end of time.'

6. GIRO D'ITALIA DIARY: WEEK 3

Richard Moore

Monday, 22 May

Rest day, Bergamo

The first stop on my return to the Giro is Hotel Spampatti, where Cannondale-Drapac are staying, high in the mountains overlooking the Conca della Presolana valley, part of the Presolona ski resort. The air is thin and cool and the vibe is very Cannondale. I am here mainly to see Joe Dombrowski, who is sitting outside wearing Birkenstock sandals and sipping herbal tea in the company of Matt Beaudin, the team's press officer. Matt is drinking beer.

I'm also here to see Michael 'Rusty' Woods. We sit outside and talk about his running career – Woods remains the fastest Canadian to run a mile on Canadian soil, though injuries ended what looked like becoming a glittering career – and his late switch to cycling. Now thirty, he is making his Grand Tour debut at the Giro – and *loving* it. His enthusiasm is unusual and endearing; he can't wait for the big mountain stages to come. After about ten minutes Matt raises his hand – usually the cue to finish.

'Ah,' I say, 'I think Matt wants me to let you go to dinner.'

'No, no,' Matt shouts across, 'I was just going to tell you to ask him about Hawaii and how he came to JV's [Jonathan Vaughters'] attention.'

After the interview, Joe and I go for a drive in the Maserati. Like many pro bike riders, Joe likes cars and likes to drive extremely fast. On the hairpins of the mountain, where we almost achieve lift-off, he offers a demonstration of what the car is capable of. It feels as though up until now we have been driving with the handbrake on. It's the fastest I have ever been in a car driven by someone wearing sandals.

Tuesday, 23 May

Stage 16: Rovetta–Bormio, 222km
Stage winner: Vincenzo Nibali
Pink jersey: Tom Dumoulin

Well, well. There are stages when something happens and the instant you see it, you know you'll be talking about it for years. Chris Froome running up Mont Ventoux in the 2016 Tour de France was one such moment. And now we can add Tom Dumoulin crapping at the base of the Stelvio.

Mid-stage, the race leader slows down, stops, begins peeling off his clothes . . . we are literally seconds from seeing him squat by the roadside when the TV director mercifully cuts back to the group with the other overall contenders. To a man they look confused. Should they wait, or press on? The Stelvio is coming up, the focal point of the stage, perhaps the entire Giro; there's a break up the road, it contains Steven Kruijswijk, among others . . .

You don't see this kind of thing often but there are precedents. In the 1986 Tour de France Greg LeMond had diarrhoea and relieved himself in a teammate's hat, tossing it into the bushes. At the finish, in his team's campervan, he had to go again, this time in a box of postcards bearing the image of his teammate, Bernard Hinault. Given that Hinault became his bitter rival later in the race, it was poetic.

On the flight back over to Italy I had read, in Herbie Sykes' new book, *Giro 100*, a new take on an older story. During the 1957 Giro Charly Gaul, when he stopped to answer a call of nature, was attacked by Louison Bobet and others – it arguably cost Gaul the race and gave him a hated nickname, *Monsieur Pee-pee*. That much I knew. What I didn't know was that the whole thing was a trap. Gaul's teammate, Aurelio Cestari, told Sykes that Bobet did indeed stop for a pee, 'Only Bobet didn't actually need to pee.' Bobet stopped only to try and trick Gaul into stopping. Then, 'His brother Jean gave the sign – a whistle – and at that point you knew it was full gas. Charly was left there on the side of the road, and his pink jersey disappeared into the distance.' Ah, the 1950s. A golden era.

Dumoulin's impromptu stop is extraordinary. We watch in disbelief as, business completed (with the help of toilet paper supplied by the Orica-Scott team car, we learn later), he re-mounts and chases. Never mind Dumoulin's shorts, by now the gloves are off up front. This will be the focus of the discussion later – in fact, it will become a theme of the season: did Dumoulin's rivals break one of cycling's unwritten rules by attacking the pink jersey when he suffered misfortune? Can it be called misfortune? It was hardly a crash or a puncture. I guess one way of looking at it is to say that having the leader's jersey offers some insurance; it affords special privileges (whether it should or not is another debate). But like most insurance policies, not everything is covered. Insurance policies usually contain an 'Act of God' clause, protecting the insurer against massive payouts in the event of a natural disaster. Surely this is exactly what befell Dumoulin: a natural disaster, rendering his insurance policy (as conferred by the pink jersey) invalid. His rivals were right to carry on.

We discuss the Dumoulin epoo-sode on the podcast. Well, I say discuss. I hadn't realised how averse Daniel is to anything of a scatological nature. I know now. We move on swiftly, on this occasion to wonderful lodgings: the Altavilla Locanda, on the outskirts of Bianzone. It's a restaurant with rooms (*locanda*: inn; don't get Daniel started on the differences between a *locanda*, an *osteria*, *trattoria*, etc.), perched on a hill just outside the village. Despite the remote location, the roads around it are reassuringly packed with cars. It's heaving inside; we get the last table and ask for the local speciality, buckwheat pizzoccheri. As we take in our surroundings we realise we are in the vicinity of some distinguished diners: Maurizio Fondriest, looking as lean as the day he won the 1988 world road race; and at another table, a white-haired, well-dressed gentleman in the company of two women. Daniel recognises him and just as he's about to tell me who it is, the man starts singing. It's quite strange. Or it would be, if the avuncular fellow wasn't Dino Zandegù, 1967 Tour of Flanders winner, four-time Giro stage winner, and a singer of some distinction, whose Giro-themed songs used to have a nightly slot on RAI. Later, as we clear our plates of deliciously creamy pasta, Daniel asks Dino for another song. I press record on my iPhone, nudging the device towards the edge of the table as Dino launches into a medley about the Giro, Nibali, Quintana . . . We will open the following night's podcast with our secret recording.

I only knew Zandegù from Daniel's biography of Eddy Merckx, *The Cannibal*, where he is the source of some memorable stories (especially, as he told Daniel, later in the afternoon, once he has started on the wine). His take on Merckx: 'He came at us from every angle, slaughtered every one of us, like some rabid wild man, some barbarian . . . ' Zandegù used to burst into song back then, too, sometimes at Merckx's request.

Another story he told Daniel was about a 1971 criterium in Modigliana, on a hilly circuit. When Merckx could not drop him, Zandegù sat on his wheel, incurring the wrath of Eddy: 'Pull! Pull, you good-for-nothing.' Merckx called Zandegù 'all the names under the sun' and told him that 'he'll see to it that I never race again if I do the sprint'. The prize is 'a golden hen that's worth quite a lot of money.' Zandegù sprints, and wins. 'Five metres beyond the finish line, I spot a gap in the crowd, turn off the road and down this little gravel path. At the end of the path is a house. I jump off my bike, sling it over my shoulder, burst through the open door of the house and run upstairs into one of the bedrooms. An old woman is there in her bed. I wake her and she starts shrieking. I say "Granny, granny, be quiet! I won't hurt you, but Eddy Merckx is coming after me and he wants to rip my face off!"'

By the way, the reason for secretly recording Zandegù didn't owe to any concern that he might decline to perform. *Au contraire*: we were worried that if he knew we were recording, he wouldn't stop. The next day, I see him at the stage finish performing for a small audience. When eventually he pauses, I ask for a selfie.

Richard with Dino Zandegù

Wednesday, 24 May

Stage 17: Tirano–Canazei, 219km
Stage winner: Pierre Rolland
Pink jersey: Tom Dumoulin

We may have mentioned on the podcast, once or twice, that the Cannondale-Drapac team has been suffering a drought: no World Tour wins for over two years. The Giro brought this into sharp focus because it was at this race, on 12 May 2015, that Davide Formolo got their last win. The drought ended six days ago when Andrew Talansky won a stage of the Tour of California. But still. In Europe the wait goes on. There is a beleaguered air around the team.

Today is a classic transitional stage between the Alps and the Dolomites. A three-star stage, according to the organisers, sandwiched between two five-star ones. Lumpy, rather than mountainous. The run-in to the finish in Canazei, which we drive on pretty, but choked-up roads, is undulating and gradually uphill. We drive past Dave Brailsford, riding the end of the stage. Five minutes later, he passes us as we sit in traffic. It's like commuting in London.

Twenty-plus riders are in the day's break, among them Pierre Rolland and Michael Woods from Cannondale. The strongest rider looks to be Valerio Conti, a young Italian of great promise, riding today like an eager puppy. He does too much. He goes too early. When caught, he goes again. With everyone watching Conti, it's the perfect moment for someone else to slip away. Which is exactly what Rolland, with 7km left, does. And he churns a huge gear all the way to the finish, while Woods rides like a seasoned pro behind, jumping on anything that moves. Rolland wins the stage.

We leave the finish almost immediately to go to the Cannondale hotel only a few kilometres back down the valley. We arrive as they are gathering amid bottles of champagne, embraces and tears. You realise, on occasions like this, how invested everyone – mechanics, *soigneurs*, physios, bus driver – is in the fortunes of the team. The one person missing is Rolland, the victor. He will arrive later, after all the stuff that follows a win: podium, interviews, dope control.

Daniel and I speak to *directeur sportif* Charly Wegelius, but it isn't easy to find the right tone. We say congratulations but of course we are there to observe rather than to share in their success. Wegelius appears more relieved than happy. The pressure on him, even implicitly, must have been enormous. He makes a quip to that effect: 'If I was a football manager I'd have been sacked a long time ago, wouldn't I?' But he is grimacing rather than smiling. As we watch him greet old friends who have come to the hotel to meet him (he spent most of his professional career in Italy), I notice that he is shaking.

Thursday, 25 May

Stage 18: Moena–Ortisei–St Ulrich, 137km
Stage winner: Tejay van Garderen
Pink jersey: Tom Dumoulin

Hands down this is the most beautiful stage I've ever driven in a Grand Tour. We set off through Canazei, where yesterday's stage finished, and then begin, at a point I can't really determine, to climb the Pordoi Pass, winding up through the trees, emerging on a plateau and stopping at a restaurant that stands there all alone. It's magical: the light, the colours, the sense of being somewhere 'other'. The Alps might be like this if there were no people and it wasn't so over-developed. But it still wouldn't be as lovely on the eye, and it's difficult to imagine the air being as pure ('I was first over the summit there five times,' said Fausto Coppi of the Pordoi Pass, 'maybe because whenever I was in that area I could breathe beautifully'). The road itself, transporting us through pine forest to this point, is sheer pleasure: 27 hairpins over 11.8km to an elevation of 2,239 metres. It's not ridiculously steep, at most 8 per cent, making it enjoyable to drive – and, I can (sort of) easily imagine, cycle.

The Dolomites themselves, as Daniel has often told us, are distinctively attractive. There aren't the jagged peaks of the Alps and Pyrenees; they are rounded, like giant volcanic plugs, or great lumps of coral, with the same smoothed off, worn-down quality. I am sort of stealing here from the best description I could find, which is in Daniel's

A view of the mountains from Valtellina in Lombardy

(wonderful!) paean to the mountains, *Mountain High*, which in turn was quoting Alexander Robertson in his 1903 book, *Through the Dolomites*: 'They resemble reefs, over which may have broken, throughout long ages, the billows of an angry ocean.'

Brilliant.

At the restaurant there's one other vehicle in the car park: the gleaming white Skoda of *L'Équipe* with that familiar logo – tall, red, gently slanting capital letters – emblazoned on the side. It is, as Daniel notes, one of the great brands. But something else struck me as we approached the car park and spotted the *L'Équipe* car sitting there, all alone: the timelessness of this image. I could imagine the *L'Équipe* car stopping here during a 1960s Giro, its journalists and their driver inside the café sipping their coffee and smoking their Gauloises. That's something else that hasn't changed about *L'Équipe*: they still have a driver to ferry the writers and keep the car looking immaculate. The journalists here are Gilles Simon, the cycling editor, and Philippe Brunel, with his shoulder-length black hair, who wears the same outfit every day: skinny black jeans and tight black T-shirt, sometimes with a (black) pullover slung around his neck, as is compulsory for Frenchmen of a certain age. He is sixty-one, but could be in his mid-forties. He's been writing about cycling for thirty-eight years. Today the three of them sit at an outside table with their driver, drinking coffee, not smoking, but doing something almost as bad for a Frenchman's health: discussing the prospects of Thibaut Pinot.

Daniel says he's having an espresso and asks if I want one. I check my watch: 11.30a.m. 'Cappuccino, please,' I say, anticipating Daniel's scowl in response. If I had dropped my trousers and done a Dumoulin in the middle of the floor, he couldn't look more disgusted.

Friday, 26 May

Stage 19: Innichen–Piancavallo, 191km
Stage winner: Mikel Landa
Pink jersey: Nairo Quintana

Daniel loses it today. In the Piancavallo ski resort we eat the press buffet in a large, open bar area, where TV screens show the stage. Daniel is very quiet and keeps glancing over his shoulder. He's distracted, preoccupied – troubled, I'd say. Eventually, leaning in, he whispers: 'Tonkov.'

'What?'

'Next table. Pavel Tonkov. Childhood hero.'

The boyish Tonkov, instantly recognisable for his cheekbones, is sitting in jeans and trainers, man bag slung over his shoulder. He's forty-eight but looks about eighteen. A great advert for the diet of a 1990s professional cyclist. Ahem. Tonkov won the Giro in 1996 and it was the Giro, perhaps because he mainly rode for Italian teams, that showcased his talent and his class. He's best known for his head-to-heads with Marco Pantani: they were a contrast in styles, Pantani swashbuckling and attacking, in and out of the saddle; Tonkov, always seated, grinding it out, but smooth as silk. Still, it is unusual for a millennial (as Daniel very nearly is) to favour Tonkov over Pantani. Then again, Daniel is unusual.

I imagine that teenagers these days would be similarly smitten by Mikel Landa. Finally, at the third time of asking, the Basque wins a stage. In Bormio he was mugged by Vincenzo Nibali and in Ortisei, in almost identical fashion, by Tejay van Garderen. To be beaten in a two-up sprint by Nibali is fair enough – the Shark knows how to race and how to win. I'm not saying that Van Garderen doesn't – OK, I am – but Landa made a right mess of that one. Today, not wanting to risk a third embarrassment, he attacks on the climb and wins alone at Piancavallo. His consistency and strength in this final week has many of us wondering how he'd have got on if he hadn't been caught in the crash twelve days ago on the stage to Blockhaus. So much for What ifs. In the actual race for the pink jersey, Dumoulin suffers a setback, losing contact and conceding the *maglia rosa* to Quintana. Finely balanced until now, it looks like the Giro might be tilting towards the Colombian.

Saturday, 27 May

Stage 20: Pordenone–Asiago, 190km
Stage winner: Thibaut Pinot
Pink jersey: Nairo Quintana

An unusual assignment this morning. Two, in fact. Unfortunately, it means an early start and departure from our lovely hotel, on a golf course, where we enjoyed a drink the previous evening with the Eurosport crew.

The first task is to drive over to the Dimension Data team hotel to meet their principal, Doug Ryder. Ryder has agreed to one of the in-car interviews that we're contractually obliged to do. That makes it sound like a chore; in fact, we haven't encountered too much opposition to our proposals of an interview in, and perhaps a turn behind the wheel of, the Maserati.

The funny thing is, these interviews tend to yield more. Maybe it's the distraction of the car, the movement; the fact that, when we're driving, or being driven, the mind wanders. People open up and talk more freely. First impressions are good when the diminutive Ryder gets in the car and moves the seat back, joking that he must be taller than Mark Cavendish (an earlier passenger). If he feels that he can make a joke about Cavendish's height then he must be (a) relaxed and (b) confident that I won't repeat it (at least not for several months. And in a book. I'm sure it'll be fine).

With Ryder dropped back at his hotel, the second task of the morning is to deliver a Pédaleur de Charme T-shirt to Tom Dumoulin. It's dreadful timing. 'Terribly sorry about you losing the pink jersey yesterday, Tom – but here's a nice T-shirt.'

The public have voted him the winner, however, and we cannot ignore the will of the people. The only option is to doorstep him at his hotel. I wait in the lobby, on a sofa near the lift. After about twenty minutes the lift opens and three zebras emerge – the Sunweb riders in their kit, ready to ride to the start. While two of them turn left and head for the entrance, Dumoulin, with a sense of urgency, turns right and heads towards me. He looks distracted. I stand up, but think better of interrupting him as he flops his bag down on the sofa where I'd just been sitting. Already half open, it falls completely open, revealing chaos. 'Fuck, fuck,' he says, digging through his stuff. 'Fuck.'

'Everything OK?' I ask.

'I've lost . . . I can't find . . . Oh, never mind.' (It was a headphones crisis, I am later told.)

'Well, um, Tom, it might not be the best moment, but I have something for you.' The big reveal: I unfurl the T-shirt. 'Our listeners have voted you our Pédaleur de Charme for the final week of the Giro.'

'Oh, thanks. Thanks, that's cool.'

He actually looks quite pleased as he takes the creased garment and smiles for a picture before stuffing it in his bag. I hope he is more careful with his T-shirt than he was with his headphones.

Giro Pédaleur de Charme, Tom Dumoulin

Later, no doubt buoyed by his victory in our Pédaleur de Charme competiton and with the help of riders on rival teams, Dumoulin gives himself a good chance of winning the Giro in Milan tomorrow. And Pinot finally gets a well-deserved stage win. For a brief moment, our French colleagues at *L'Équipe* look happy.

Sunday, 28 May

Stage 21: Monza–Milan, 29.3km
Stage winner: Jos van Emden
Pink jersey: Tom Dumoulin

Tom Dumoulin has given us some wonderful stories and – almost as importantly from our point of view – great lines. 'I'm not here to make history for shitting in the bushes,' as he eloquently put it before the final stage. 'I'm here to write history for taking the pink jersey to Milan.'

It's strange driving into Milan for the final stage because, on the one hand, we expect Dumoulin to win. But on the other, it still seems quite unlikely. The reason is simply that he is fourth, albeit only 53 seconds down. Nobody has ever leapfrogged three riders on the final day to win a Grand Tour before. But the final stage of the 1989 Tour de France – when Greg LeMond surprised Laurent Fignon to wipe out a 50-second deficit over 24.5km – this ain't. On the 29.3km course, starting on the motor racing circuit in Monza, Dumoulin looks the probable winner pretty much from the first pedal-stroke. It is never in doubt.

Final days of Grand Tours can feel flat and underwhelming. This one doesn't. The Piazza Duomo, with the podium set up to the side of the cathedral, is a beautiful setting as millions of pink ribbons are blasted into Milan's azure sky and Dumoulin calls his Sunweb teammates forward to join him on a stage that extends into the crowds. There are probably more Colombians packed into the Piazza, but the Dutch make themselves heard, singing their new anthem, 'Tommy Du-moulin, Du-moulin, To-o-o-o-o-mmy Du-moulin,' to the tune of KC and the Sunshine Band's *Give It Up*. Very Dutch. But in all the celebrations, one aspect is overlooked by pretty much everyone – and could become a pub quiz question in Holland: who won the time trial into

Milan on the final day of the 2017 Giro? Such was Dumoulin's strength in time trials in this Giro it seems inconceivable that it was a Dutchman, but not him.

Yet it was.

Step forward, Jos van Emden. A great stage win, but a terrible stage to win.

For captions, see page 246

7. A TALE OF TWO TOURS

Ashleigh Moolman Pasio

Ashleigh Moolman Pasio

It was something I automatically wanted. That was the pinnacle, that was our yellow jersey and this was our Tour de France. I could feel the energy of the event channelling through my stomach, making me feel my nerves. I felt like more of a spectator than an athlete as I tried to look like I knew what I was doing. Of course, I could ride a bike but this was more than balancing and pedalling. The world's best female cyclists were here, with big teams, and big legs. Did I mention big legs? I had ambitions to wear the pink leader's jersey and win the tour overall but it was my first Giro Rosa and I was a nobody, invisible in the bunch.

I just wanted to stay out of trouble and see what the climbs could bring . . . and finish the whole tour. The first stage that year, in 2010, was 58km from Muggia to Trieste and I finished in the main bunch, 18 seconds down on Ina Teutenberg, officially in 101st place. It wasn't until Stage 5 that the road turned up and I saw some light. The real race between the leaders and the favourites was up the road in front of me but, a minute behind them, I was leading a group of six up the climb to the line. That was the story for the rest of the race. I wasn't in the mix but I was following it, always chasing to just be in sight. I finished 17th.

The next year I was 13th, then 12th, 8th, and 4th. From bunch filler to GC contender, I had gone from worrying about being dropped to planning attacks. I hadn't worn the pink jersey but I had sprinted for stage wins, led a team, and worn the polka-dot jersey. Along the way I had also won races, a Commonwealth medal, and represented South Africa at the Olympics twice. I had raced with the best and become one of the best, but when I lined up for the 2017 Giro ready and able to fight for the podium, I realised my adoration of the pink jersey had faded.

The pink jersey had represented a lot to me. When I started it was our equivalent of the yellow jersey in the Tour de France. The Giro was our only 'Grand Tour', and as the longest and hardest stage race on the women's calendar, the leader's jersey symbolised the toughest prize to be won. While our jersey wasn't as world renowned as the men's yellow jersey, in the small arena of women's cycling it was considered the most prestigious jersey you could win. You couldn't just be one of the best to win it, you had to be the best of the best.

It was so far out of reach at my first Giro but the closer I got, the more I saw the reality. My desire to win the race was stronger than ever but something had changed. The prestige of pink was tarnished by awful food, crappy hotels, lacklustre routes, poor prize money, and practically no marketing of the event. The lack of coverage was beyond frustrating, bordering on the comical, and the fact that we raced during the Tour de France was either a curse or an opportunity but no one from the organisation seemed to care either way. Outside the small world of women's cycling, no one seemed to know about the Giro, let alone the pink jersey.

Part of me realised I had just grown out of it. Not the leader's jersey but the actual race. I wasn't young and naïve and blinded by the simple opportunity to race. My tolerance for poor treatment (and cold plain pasta) had worn thin. On top of everything, the UCI points for the overall win were the equivalent of a one-day race. The investment required to show up to the Giro, let alone perform, was astronomical in comparison. From the physical and mental training to the logistics and wherewithal, according to my calculations, the end did not justify the means.

I had to check my maths, though. It seemed somewhat arrogant to colour our Tour de France this way but I ran the numbers again and it just didn't add up. How was the Giro surviving? Why were women's teams still willing to show up? I wasn't the only one starting to ask questions. The points issue had been brought up on cycling news outlets and a few other riders brought up a range of issues on podcasts, not to mention the chatter in the bunch. That's when I realised it wasn't the fact that I had changed, it was that the race hadn't changed. And was never going to change.

No longer did I think it was OK for the 'most prestigious' tour to serve us plain pasta every meal (and I mean every single meal). No longer did I think it was OK to jam riders into cars for upwards of four-hour transfers between stages. No longer did I think it was OK to sleep in dormitories or dirty, old hotels. No longer did I think it was acceptable to have no race results published, no coverage of any kind, laughable prize money, disproportionate UCI points . . . I understand many races, including the Giro, have seemingly impossible budgets, but that's not a good enough reason any more. The pink jersey now represented the past, but it wasn't just me that had grown out of it, so had women's cycling.

In the seven years since my first Giro, women's cycling had changed. With the increasing depth of the peloton, riders were now targeting certain races instead of being able to podium year-round. There has been an increase in professionalism among teams, the inauguration of the UCI Women's Commission, increased media exposure, and progressive changes to the calendar. While there is still a long way to go to achieve equality, we're clearly past taking what we can get.

Still, here I was on the start line of the Giro again on Friday, June 30 2017 but somewhere between abandoning on Stage 2 and getting home to Girona, I knew it was time to let go of the pink jersey. I had a long history with that race. I had planned seasons around it; I used it as the measuring stick for annual progress; it was always my big goal. I was so unskilled and inexperienced in my first edition and this year I had a shot at the overall win. A part of me would always want it and if my team wanted me to race it, I would always do my best, but the mystique was gone. Everything had come into focus and I didn't like what I saw any more. I had believed in the lore of the jersey but reality was telling a different – a true – story and, as I watched the Giro from the sidelines for the first time, it was too blatant to ignore. Actually, I couldn't watch it. There wasn't any coverage.

As I recovered from illness I knew breaking the spell was a good thing. It did matter that I had changed. I had experienced races that had responded to the changes in women's cycling, most notably the Women's Tour. The course was challenging, there was extensive media coverage, the race was supported from start to finish wherever we rode, and the food was much more varied and interesting. Just a couple of weeks before the Giro Rosa, when we had been screaming around the corners of central London on the final stage – up Regent Street, taking in Whitehall, Trafalgar Square and Piccadilly Circus – I knew we had a new Tour de France. The crowds were thick and energising. The best of the women's peloton was racing and we were putting on a show. The Women's Tour had been exciting, challenging, and professional. This is modern women's cycling.

I was surrounded by a group of powerful, ambitious people, and I'm not just talking about the peloton. I'm including the organisers and the spectators. Here was a living, breathing example of the future of our sport. The Women's Tour was adamant on progress, not only on continually improving the race for the riders with plans for additional stages and more challenging terrain, but demonstrating that a race can function successfully as a business. It was a race over five days and taking us around Great Britain, before vast crowds, including thousands of school-children, allowing riders to perform at their best and showing the world what that looked like. It was the kind of race that was building a history and equally opening the door to the future, showing race directors how to operate sustainably and inspiring the next generation (or even the current one) to hop on a bike. It was the one race on the women's calendar that deserved the appellation the women's Tour de France.

It seemed strange these two races were both on our calendar as World Tour events on a seemingly equal footing. While the Giro Rosa seemed to be resting on its laurels, the Women's Tour was working to build the future. That seemed to sum up the entire state of women's cycling: half the stakeholders are stuck in the past; half are trying to build the future.

I often hear from people that women's cycling is slow, boring, and unsellable but that assessment doesn't hold true. Look at the London 2012 women's road race — we all remember the horrific rain and the exciting chase that put women's cycling in the spotlight. Rio was equally dramatic, as was the chase up the famous Col d'Izoard at La Course. The World Championship road race in Norway was, in the opinion of Mark Cavendish, who has helped champion women's cycling, 'the most exciting of the whole week' and the 'perfect way to showcase' our sport.

It hardly fails that people who describe women's cycling negatively are searching for an excuse. Whether that's an excuse for poor planning, not watching, or refusing to change, it's always a justification for some belief or behaviour that undermines the future of the sport. That might be an unpopular opinion but change-makers hardly bow to the convention.

People laughed at me and didn't believe I would ever make it as an athlete and, yes, the odds were highly stacked against me, but there is always a path forward, always work to be done, always changes to be made to achieve a goal. I didn't start out in life with that perspective, nor as a cyclist. I was well into my engineering degree at the University of Cape

Town when things changed. The bike wasn't the point of change; it was meeting my husband Carl.

Carl was this avid, amazing athlete, who was also studying engineering. He was distracted by sport, whereas I was really good at university work, and just after we started dating we had our first exam. When we got our maths marks back we were sitting together in class. The lecturer stood at the front and said: 'The lowest mark in the class is 11 per cent and the highest mark is 90 per cent. Whoever got 11 per cent, you should really reconsider your direction of studies, and I think you should get out of this class. And whoever got 90 per cent, you're doing incredibly well, and should be proud of yourself.' She then invited us to come and get our papers and we went up, nervous, to collect them. I still remember the blank look on Carl's face as he scanned it nervously and asked me, 'What did you get?'

Before I could tell him, he noticed that I was the one with the highest mark. He dropped his paper and ran – he was the one with 11 per cent. I thought, 'Oh my word, here we go – I've chased away my boyfriend!' I set off and eventually found him in his room and knocked on his door. 'You know what,' I said, 'we can do this together. If you teach me how to ride a bike, I'll teach you how to study and do well at maths.' And that's literally how things happened. From then on, I was his maths mentor, and he was my cycling mentor.

He planted the idea that cycling was a possibility and continued to believe in me. I had participated in a few local cycling events and tried my hand at triathlon but it wasn't until Carl showed me cycling that I really took to the bike. Of course, already being in university meant I was a late starter but he always pushed me to believe in what could be. That belief, against the odds of 'making it' and counter to what seemed sensible and secure, made me believe, too. When we made the decision for me to focus on cycling and race in Europe during part of the semester (while Carl stayed behind and helped me finish my assignments), I learned what the belief in possibility could do. I had changed my goals; I had changed my life; I had a completely new perspective.

After finishing my studies in 2009, I was racing in Europe full time, trying to earn a place in the professional peloton; but I broke my collarbone not once, not twice, but three times in the space of those first twelve months. Each time was more heart-breaking than the last. The third was the hardest, especially since it cost me my first opportunity with the South African national team. I had been selected for the 2010 Commonwealth Games in Delhi, but a car turned across me on a training ride in Belgium and that was that. I remember talking to my mum after and she asked me if cycling was worth it. It was a good question. I had to rethink things but there was still so much I wanted to achieve, and that belief I had started to build nagged me to continue. If I kept going, there was the possibility I could achieve all my goals; if I stopped, none of it was possible.

There have been many times I have wanted to stop cycling and pursue other things. The crashes, disappointments, and crappy hotels start to add up. With all the sacrifices you make, and your friends and family make, sometimes it becomes overwhelming and the easiest (and often most sensible) choice would be to stop. In both failure and success, however, possibility always remains my guiding north arrow. It may not always point in the direction I want – like six months of rehab, letting go of a dream, or holding an unpopular opinion – but there is always a way forward to the goal.

That belief in possibility is a tradition in women's cycling. It may not be apparent on the surface but it's the longest standing tradition we have. It's the positive power of our sport. The challenge, the beauty, the ability to inspire and effect change; the capacity to provide opportunity, showcase the human spirit, and bring people together. Those aren't ideals, those are truths showcased in the tradition of pursuing athletic excellence. Every attack on a climb, each sprint for the line, the years of training, the wins, the losses, the team work, and the individual sacrifice. That's the tradition of women's cycling that will build the future. That's the tradition of women's cycling I believe in.

I came to realise that's what drew me to the pink jersey all those years

Ashleigh Moolman Pasio on the Mur de Huy at Flèche Wallonne

ago. It wasn't just about winning the longest and toughest race on the calendar, it was also about the celebration of our sport at the highest level. It was about the work behind winning those eight days of racing, not just in the pursuit of individual performance, but in the pursuit of pushing the sport of women's cycling to a higher level. I also realised that the prestige of the pink jersey was still alive, it just wasn't pink any more.

What the pink jersey stood for didn't belong to a race, it belonged to our sport. We have the power to decide what the most prestigious prize is by choosing to support the races we think worthy. By targeting those events that challenge us as athletes and teams to show up at our best and perform. We have the power of tradition – the belief in possibility – to shape our own future whether that's pink, red, green, or yellow.

8. TOUR DE FRANCE DIARY: WEEK 1

Richard Moore

Thursday, 29 June

Düsseldorf

Managed to get the train to the correct Ashford this time, after a bit of
confusion last year, to meet Lionel and Simon, the podcast
photographer (we must be the only podcast in the world with a
photographer). Then it's the Eurotunnel to Calais, a couple of hours'
drive to Lille, where Lionel and I pick up our rental car, leaving Simon
to get to Düsseldorf in his campervan. Four hours later, having driven
through France and Belgium and entered Germany, we reach
Düsseldorf, get flashed by a speed camera on our way into the city,*
and arrive at our hotel but miss the narrow turning into the car park.
After another lap of the block we wriggle through the narrow entrance,
unload our bags and lug them into reception, where we are greeted by a
stern woman, quite literally wagging her finger in my face. 'Have you
parked in the car park?'

Clearly a rhetorical question, because she carries on: 'No! You must
not park in the car park. You must move! Move! Now! Now! *Move!*'

---

* The ticket, when it comes, is modest, only €10, though we struggle to pay it online,
  despite repeated attempts. At the time of writing it's risen to about €90.

Welcome to Düsseldorf. Funny how first impressions can be so powerful.

Later in the evening we meet our star signing for the Tour, François Thomazeau: author, former head of sport at Reuters in France, gourmet, musician – his credentials as a musician will only gradually reveal themselves (he's also very modest). At this point we don't know François that well, though Lionel and I have always been impressed by him. A little in awe? Maybe. When we order a bottle of wine he inspects the label: 'Thirteen degrees,' he says. The fact he says 'degrees' instead of 'per cent' is literally the only flaw in his perfect, fluent English. Being British, Lionel and I neglect to correct him.

Friday, 30 June

Düsseldorf

Tonight *The Cycling Podcast* goes head-to-head with Kraftwerk in the German electronic music pioneers' home city. A dream come true. And for us, too.

While we do a live event for a hundred or so people in the Rapha pop-up store, Kraftwerk sound-check the show they'll be performing the following evening in the outdoor arena next door.

The Cycling Podcast has a lot in common with Kraftwerk, as we discovered when their transport rider was recently leaked. Like us, they stipulate the type of car (Mercedes Vitro with tinted windows, in their case) and drivers with 'a moderate driving style' and 'basic hygiene standards'. Our car rental company can't have got our transport rider because we've got an ageing people carrier with spongey suspension, sluggish acceleration, erratic Bluetooth connection, tinny speakers and large scrapes on the side.

During our event I make a couple of bold predictions. First, I speculate that Nairo Quintana could join Team Sky. Then we are asked how we think Geraint Thomas will get on. 'Can't see him doing anything,' I say. 'His season was all about the Giro. The Tour was a late plan B. Don't expect much from Geraint Thomas.'

An audience with Richard, Lionel and François in Düsseldorf

Saturday, 1 July

Stage 1: Düsseldorf, 14km time trial
Stage winner: Geraint Thomas
Yellow jersey: Geraint Thomas

Geraint Thomas wins stage 1 to take the first yellow jersey.

It's a popular victory because Thomas (any use of the overly familiar 'G' receives an automatic red card on *The Cycling Podcast*) is liked by everybody. There are riders who have done virtually nothing but think they are big stars. And there are riders who have achieved quite a lot but don't appear to think they're anything special. Thomas is in the second category.

This stage, run off beneath grey clouds and in persistent rain, reminds me of the start in Rotterdam in 2010. It was Sky's first Tour and Dave Brailsford was in a cocky mood. I don't find Brailsford as lacking in self-awareness as some of my colleagues do. But in Rotterdam Brailsford was setting himself up for a fall. As he looked ahead to the time trial he began sharing how he would have sorted out the England football team (if I recall correctly, they'd just been knocked out of something on penalties, again*). In the next breath he was talking about his cunning plan for the time trial: to put Bradley Wiggins off early, before the other favourites. Brailsford had consulted with meteorologists from the British sailing team who'd told him that it would rain later on. They were spectacularly wrong. The heaviest rain coincided exactly, to the minute, with Wiggins' ride. Brailsford was chastened. He is the opposite of that in rainy Düsseldorf seven years later when Sky place four in the top eight. Ominous.

A footnote to the stage – at least, it seems like a footnote at the time – is that Rigoberto Urán has a problem with his bike, which is deemed illegal just before the start. He changes to his spare and negotiates the wet streets and treacherous corners, which end the Tour for Alejandro Valverde, who suffers a horrible high-speed crash, to finish in a time a minute-and-a-half down on Thomas. For the Mick Jagger of pro cycling (and Urán has recently seemed as far from his prime as the Rolling Stones) the setback seems of no real consequence.

Oh, and it's Lionel's birthday, so we go out for a nice meal in a Polish restaurant. But Lionel is distracted, still mulling over a comment made by Mark Cavendish as he rode past having done his time trial. Approaching from behind, Cavendish casually remarked: 'I knew that was you, Lionel – you've got the weirdest walk in cycling.'

A nice bottle of 13-degree wine helps him get over this curious insult.

---

*   I think this was a 4–1 loss to Germany in Bloemfontein . . .

Sunday, 2 July

Stage 2: Düsseldorf–Liège, 203.5km
Stage winner: Marcel Kittel
Yellow jersey: Geraint Thomas

We leave Germany having not really felt the love. I expected so much –
I remember on a previous visit to Germany, in 2009, streets packed
ten-deep with spectators, and even some bunting long before Yorkshire
covered itself in the stuff in 2014 – but in Düsseldorf there seemed no
great warmth for the Tour. The weather didn't help.

Before stage 1 I meet Connie Carpenter-Phinney and Davis Phinney,
the parents of Taylor, making his Tour debut. Connie was the 1984
Olympic road race champion – the first time there was a women's road
race – while Davis was a professional, one of the American pioneers
with the 7-Eleven team, who won two stages of the Tour. These days,
Davis suffers from Parkinson's disease. It slows his movements and slurs
his speech but his mind is as alert as when, as a sprinter, he used to
dive through gaps in the blink of an eye. I ask him if he still rides his
bike and he nods. 'We try to ride our bikes every day,' says Connie.

Taylor is an interesting character and has no doubt earned vastly
more money in his career than both parents put together, but his
palmarès, to put it bluntly, is not a patch on theirs. He suffered a
terrible crash a couple of years earlier, which hasn't helped. But on his
first proper day at the Tour he makes an impression: he is in the break,
takes the king of the mountains jersey, and, with Yoann Offredo,
another debutant (and another interesting character), almost holds off
the bunch. Theirs is not a typical doomed breakaway: both are strong,
and fully committed, and they are urged on. It is not to be: they are
swept up in the final kilometre.

Consolation comes in our lodgings in Tongeren, an idyllic Flemish
village 30km from grey, industrial Liège. We eat Belgian bolognaise in

the local, no-frills restaurant, which is homely and packed, then retire to our B&B and to a fridge packed with Belgian beer. A note on the door explains that it's an honesty bar. Or a dishonesty bar, jokes Lionel. At least . . .* We sample a couple, which is dangerous with Belgian beer, since it can be as strong as 10 degrees.

Monday, 3 July

Stage 3: Verviers–Longwy, 212.5km
Stage winner: Peter Sagan
Yellow jersey: Geraint Thomas

Good stage. Dreadful hotel. Weird restaurant.

We are the only diners in the restaurant, a place trying really hard, but failing, much to François's evident disapproval. He says it's the sort of place that's busy on Sundays, with locals who dress up for the occasion, simply because there is nowhere else to go. What he says about the chef is unprintable. Culinary crimes are taken very seriously in France.

Simon orders steak. What arrives is very odd indeed. The shape and texture suggest that it might be a bull's heart. Simon pokes and prods, shoving it around his plate, before picking up his camera and scrolling through the pictures he'd taken at the finish in Longwy. The stage ended with a climb that eliminated the pure sprinters and left Peter Sagan, Greg Van Avermaet and Michael Matthews to duke it out. Simon mentions that he had a great vantage point, high on a terrace about 250 metres from the line.

We discuss Sagan's win. It was virtuoso stuff, we agreed. He made it look easy. How does he do it, we wondered. 'You wouldn't even realise that he pulled his foot out with about 250 metres to go,' I say.

'He pulled his foot out with 250 metres to go?' asks Simon, glancing

---

* Obviously, we paid in full.

up from his camera, then glancing back down to study the screen more urgently. 'Oh, Christ,' he says, holding his camera at arm's length, like a dirty nappy.

Simon, unbeknownst to him, got *the* shot. It captures the precise moment that Sagan, a length or two up, pulls his foot out. In the next frame the foot is back in. Simon, in his haste to pack up, drive to his hotel and eat (or rather, not eat) in this disappointing restaurant, had overlooked it. Now he worries that the moment has passed. In the old days he would have had good reason to be annoyed: a front-page picture discovered too late for the front pages. But in the digital age there are no such deadlines (or front pages). The picture goes out and it doesn't really matter that it's a few hours after the event: it is, after all, *the* picture of the stage, capturing a moment of real, split-second drama and telling so much about Sagan: his skill, quick-thinking and ability to improvise – but most of all, his strength.

The discovery almost makes up for the inedible bull's heart.

Tuesday, 4 July

Stage 4: Mondorf-les-Bains–Vittel, 207.5km
Stage winner: Arnaud Démare
Yellow jersey: Geraint Thomas

With the stage finishing in Vittel and us staying in nearby Contrexeville, home of Contrex water, we are in Water Central. It's a miracle we stay dry. An admission: I had never heard of Contrex water until François and Lionel embark on a long discussion about its merits, or otherwise, over dinner. François tells us about its distinctive taste, and that he cannot drink it in his favourite aperitif, pastis.

Like a powerful torrent, or a dropped hose, the discussion rages on, rushing into channels and inlets I had never imagined possible in a conversation about water. Can François really tell one brand of mineral water from another? Yes, he insists. Lionel sets a blind taste challenge. François accepts.

Today was dramatic, but it all happened in the final 200 metres. Poor Guillaume Van Keirsbulck, who attacked at the start, expecting others to follow. Nobody did. So on he went, into a headwind, for almost 200km.

In some of the stage reports the following day there is no mention of Van Keirsbulck. Not a word. Imagine riding 190km alone at the front at the Tour de France and not being mentioned? It's almost as if it didn't happen. When Van Keirsbulck arrived at the finish, almost four minutes down, he might have expected some kind of welcome. But the Tour's centre of gravity had shifted; the media were elsewhere, outside Mark Cavendish's Dimension Data bus, or Peter Sagan's Bora-Hansgrohe bus (a few, including François, were outside the FDJ bus of Arnaud Démare, the stage winner, though nobody was too bothered about him, either).

Sagan and Cavendish had collided in the finishing straight, Cavendish going for a gap that was closing, Sagan appearing to close it with his elbow. Down went Cavendish. Out – sensationally – went Sagan.

To be honest, I missed all of it. I was at the Wanty-Groupe Gobert bus waiting for Van Keirsbulck. The small Belgian team's veteran sports director Hilaire Van der Schueren sat on the step of the bus eating a baguette, spilling most of it down his shirt. I was astonished to realise, on looking up his age, that Van der Schueren is only sixty-nine. He is the very definition of old school – as long as the school is Belgian. On the eve of the Tour he sent a text message to his nine riders, all Tour debutants: 'No women in the rooms!' (The surprise for me was that he uses a mobile phone.)

I wonder how he works with his young team leader, Guillaume Martin, who I speak to at the finish. Martin is a twenty-four-year-old Frenchman with a masters degree in philosophy and an interest in Nietzsche who is writing a column for *Le Monde*. He also wrote a play. 'It's about Plato,' he tells me. 'Basically, it's the duality between the intellectual life and the life in action. It sounds serious, but it's a funny play.'

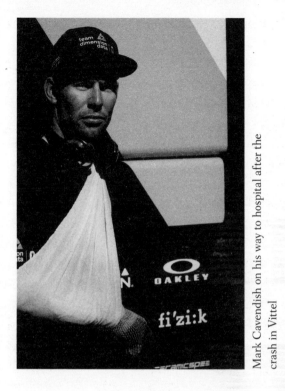

Mark Cavendish on his way to hospital after the crash in Vittel

Eventually Van Keirsbulck appears. 'I looked behind me,' he says, 'but nobody followed. I was flicked. I thought "Shit, I'll go back", but it looks stupid to go back.'

Wednesday, 5 July

Stage 5: Vittel–La Planche des Belles Filles, 160.5km
Stage winner: Fabio Aru
Yellow jersey: Chris Froome

April, 2017:
Me: 'I got us a bargain the night of the first mountain stage: €130 for three rooms. Looks OK, too.'

Lionel: 'Is that the La Planche des Belles Filles stage?'

'Yes.'

'Is it in Lure?'

'Now you mention it, yes – yes, it is in Lure.'

'Hmmm. You don't remember Lure, do you?'

Three months later it comes back to me. We stayed here in 2012, the night of a stage won by Chris Froome, where Bradley Wiggins took the first yellow jersey of his career. But all that was overshadowed by the worst hotel, the worst meal, and the most dismal experience of any Tour. As Lionel says, this corner of eastern France is struggling economically. Lure seems to epitomise the struggle.

The Tour, of course, is supposed to showcase the best of France. You can do some Tours and come away believing that the entire country is an idyll with its vast, gently rolling countryside, fields of towering sunflowers, spectacular mountains, and the Most Beautiful City in the World™, Paris. I have been seduced, returning in a state of awe, wondering how a country can be so perfect. Well – SPOILER ALERT – France is not perfect. It is probably good to be reminded occasionally.

We turn off the main thoroughfare and drive down a residential street with large, crumbling mansions set back from the road. Their grandeur offers a sense of what Lure once was. We turn into ours. I ring the bell. A child answers then runs away. There are some people out the back, so I wander round. They're on holiday, they explain, adding that there's a German gentleman in charge.

When our host appears he is friendly, slightly manic. He has a vague awareness of who has booked to stay, and who is with whom. Colleagues from *Le Monde* are arriving later, I tell him. I was just making conversation, but from this moment on he cannot be convinced of the fact that we are not together – he seems desperate for us to be one party. 'No,' I say, 'we are all journalists, but we are not together.' Each attempt at clarification only deepens the confusion. He asks if Lionel and I are a couple. Lionel shudders.

Clearly he has overbooked and doesn't have enough rooms. We are shown into an annex which will be nice when it is finished – there is exposed concrete, wires hanging from sockets, doors missing. 'You will eat,' he says – not a question. 'Barbecue!' he adds, pointing to an open fire in the garden. Lionel notices that he is missing a finger.

Although our host is friendly and eager to please, Lionel cannot be persuaded that he did not chop off his finger while preparing our barbecue. So we walk into town and eat grisly meat at the same restaurant where we'd eaten, equally miserably, five years earlier. We chew over the stage, which proves more nourishing. Fabio Aru jumped away on the climb to win, which offers some hope for the race. Sky either underestimated Aru or couldn't bring him back. We also talk, with a sense of wonder, about the day's main event – François's ability to correctly identify four different brands of water – Vittel, Evian, Volvic and Contrex – in our blind taste challenge.

François's extraordinary blind water challenge

When we return to the château, our colleagues from *Le Monde*, who arrived while we were out, are quite literally licking their fingers, patting their stomachs and purring with satisfaction. 'Where were you?' they ask. 'The barbecue was amazing – big steaks, absolutely delicious.'

They'll not be smiling when they realise they're sharing a bed.

There was very little alluring about Lure

Thursday, 6 July

Stage 6: Vesoul–Troyes, 216km
Stage winner: Marcel Kittel
Yellow jersey: Chris Froome

At the finish in Troyes I see a stocky old man with white, bushy hair chatting to Team Sky's coach, Rod Ellingworth. He is Jack Andre,

retired hairdresser and local cycling luminary. For more than forty
years he's run one of the clubs in Troyes, UVC Aube, mentoring dozens
of British riders, including Robert Millar, Malcolm Elliott, Ellingworth,
Jeremy Hunt, and most recently Adam Yates. Yet he doesn't speak a
word of English.

I met Jack a decade earlier when I went to Troyes while researching
my book, *In Search of Robert Millar*. He took me to his house, with its
impressive collection of Scotch whisky, and then to the garage: a
treasure trove of cycling memorabilia dominated by a huge picture of
Fausto Coppi. Beside it was a photograph of Millar, signed in a corner:
'To Jack Andre, a friend for life.' Jack gave me my favourite quote about
Millar: 'Robert was like a little cockerel. He liked to stand out, but he
hated people chasing him.'

I always think of Millar when the Tour comes to Troyes. Just before
we record the day's podcast, to discuss a stage won once again by
Marcel Kittel, a headline catches my eye: 'A statement from
Cyclingnews contributor Philippa York.' For several years now Robert
Millar has been living as Philippa York. It's good that, despite efforts
by tabloid newspapers, she has been able to reveal this at a time
of her choosing. It's also nice to see, as we will over the coming
days, that the response from the cycling world is so positive and
supportive.

As well as Robert Millar and Jack Andre, mention of Troyes conjures
andouillette, the sausage made from the small intestines of a pig, a
local speciality. Lionel professes to hate it ('a verruca sock filled with
rubber bands') yet has a weird obsession with it. Tonight we eat in a
lovely restaurant in the centre of Troyes. Simon, thinking that nothing
can be worse than his Longwy steak, orders it. So does François, of
course. When it arrives, François inhales and tucks in, insisting it's
delicious. Again, Simon pokes and prods and moves it around his plate
before hiding it beneath a lettuce leaf.

On the way back to our hotel we bump into Christian Prudhomme,
the charismatic Tour director, with Philippe Sudres, the ever-present

Andouillette, which translates as 'disgusting sausage'

communications director who has worked for the Tour since the early 1980s. Prudhomme is remarkable, a force of nature. It's gone midnight yet here he is, in trademark chinos, the sleeves of his sky blue shirt rolled up, standing outside a bar, still at the centre of it all, laughing and joking and enjoying a glass of wine, or eight.

'At the Tour he has to go to the best restaurant in town for dinner with the mayor,' says François of Prudhomme's schedule. 'Or should I say, best restaurants; sometimes he has two or three dinners.' François, who studied journalism with Prudhomme, tells us how he does it: that Prudhomme follows his predecessor Jean-Marie Leblanc's old rule, 'twelve weeks on the booze, six weeks off.'

'Or so he says,' François adds, 'but I have seen him drinking wine at the Vuelta.'

Friday, 7 July

Stage 7: Troyes–Nuits-Saint-Georges, 213.5km
Stage winner: Marcel Kittel
Yellow jersey: Chris Froome

The knowledge that we are staying in probably the best hotel of the Tour adds a certain urgency to our day. That, and the knowledge that another flat stage almost inevitably means another Marcel Kittel win – though it's close, because he is almost caught out by Edvald Boasson Hagen.

The photo gives it to Kittel, but Boasson Hagen, ever since his teammate Cavendish went home, has been thriving. There's never been any doubt about his talent but there have always been questions about

François's snails

his hunger. Today, after losing one of the closest stages in Tour history, Boasson Hagen says: 'Second is quite good.'

There are no such questions about our hunger and we race to our hotel, the wonderfully named La Gentilhommière. No sooner have I put my bag on my bed than I see, marching past my window, François in his swimming trunks, heading for the pool.

At dinner we spot, at a nearby table, a collection of former pros, all working for ASO: 1980s star Charly Mottet, 1984 Vuelta winner Eric Caritoux and Patrice Esnault. 'You know that you are somewhere good,' says François, 'when there are people who work for ASO eating there.'

Lionel compares the hors d'oeuvre to pork scratchings. François then starts with snails (so large and succulent he calls them Kittel snails) then moves on to lobster, as we all do, oddly, in a place that is just about the furthest point in France from the sea. But François ordered it

Charly Mottet, Pédaleur de Charme

and, well . . . anyway, the lobster is delicious, and the conversation flows like the Burgundy wine until, inevitably, we collar a bemused Mottet, and make him wear a Pédaleur de Charme *casquette*.

Saturday, 8 July

Stage 8: Dole–Station-des-Rousses, 187.5km
Stage winner: Lilian Calmejane
Yellow jersey: Chris Froome

A punk rock day, says Lionel, as fifty riders make the big break, including lots of hitters. Warren Barguil is very active, scooping up King of the Mountains points. Lilian Calmejane then goes clear but suffers a vicious attack of cramp on the final climb while being chased by Robert Gesink. 'Game over,' I say on a podcast that we're doing as-live from the top of the hill. I said this with such conviction that it was inevitable that Calmejane would recover and win the stage.

That morning, in Dole, I had waited outside his Direct Energie team bus to try and speak to Thomas Voeckler, riding his final Tour. Forget it. The crowds were enormous, as big as at any bus, and they were all there for Voeckler. When eventually he emerged he signed a few autographs and posed for some pictures but had no time to speak to me. Minutes earlier, Calmejane had pedalled off without any fuss. I could have grabbed him for a word (he speaks good English having studied briefly in the Nottingham area) but – in my first bad call concerning Calmejane today – I had bigger fish to fry, so I didn't bother. Jean-René Bernaudeau and the rest of the management at Direct Energie fancy that Calmejane will be Voeckler's successor as the team's talisman. Today seems to confirm it.

The highlight of the day, however, concerns Daniel's crowing at the finish. In *Procycling* magazine he'd tipped Calmejane for today's stage, which he took great delight in telling our listeners. Only problem was, the Nostradamus of the cycling world had written too much, and some of his precious words – including this prediction – were cut from the magazine. Poor Daniel. He was reduced to digging out the original Word doc and posting it on Twitter as evidence.

Sunday, 9 July

Stage 9: Nantua–Chambéry, 181.5km
Stage winner: Rigoberto Urán
Yellow jersey: Chris Froome

A quiet day at the Tour de France. Chris Froome has a mechanical on the Mont du Chat, sticks his arm up and drops back. As he does so, Fabio Aru attacks – under his arm! Porte then orders everyone, including Aru, to wait. When he regains contact with the group, Froome swerves, colliding with a rider on the inside and almost running him off the road. The rider is Aru.

On the descent Richie Porte has a sickening, high-speed crash. And just like that he's out. Dan Martin slams into him and falls heavily, but gets back up. He's still in.

Then Geraint Thomas crashes. He's out. Robert Gesink, too. (We breezily list the casualties, but Gesink, one day after almost winning the stage, is seriously hurt, fracturing vertebrae; when he comes round in hospital he is looking at three months off the bike.) Behind all this, Arnaud Démare is enduring his second day of utter torture. The FDJ sprinter is just trying to survive. Inexplicably, his team allocate him three teammates. They all finish outside the time limit. 'No one sent us, we saw the situation and we made a decision. We win together, we lose together,' says Ignatas Konovalovas. 'The way they rode was much more than work, it was love,' says Démare. But they are out.

The finale is bizarre. Froome is isolated, with Romain Bardet and others up the road, yet finds allies in the Astana pair, Aru and Jakob

Fuglsang. They wait three Tours for Froome to be isolated – and then help him! In the six-man sprint, Astana's deadly duo finish fifth and sixth. Well done, boys! Warren Barguil seems to win, celebrates and commences post-stage interviews when he is told that the photo shows Rigoberto Urán – oh, did I mention that Urán had problems with his gears in the final kilometres, and was down to two, a massive one and a tiny one? – had pipped him. On learning this, Barguil starts crying.

Phew. Thank God it's a rest day tomorrow.

9. THE RULES OF RACE RADIO

Sebastien Piquet

Radio Tour is the official channel – race radio – at the Tour de France, available to officials, teams and media. It is broadcast from the Chief Commissaire's car, which follows immediately behind the peloton or first group, and conveys all the essential information: crashes, punctures, the identity of riders in a breakaway, or who have been dropped. Since 2005 the voice of Radio Tour, and the man occupying the passenger seat in the lead car, has been Sebastien Piquet.

When asked to talk about my experiences as the Radio Tour speaker during the Tour de France, I'm afraid I have to admit the unadmittable. The first time I had goosebumps on my arms, a smile on my face that I was struggling to conceal, and a real vivid emotion was on a stage heading to Courchevel back in 2005. We were behind the leading group in the final kilometres: the yellow jersey group. I was in sheer admiration. Heart beating. Slightly overexcited.

And so to the unadmittable: in front of our red car were Lance Armstrong, Alejandro Valverde, Michael Rasmussen and Francisco Mancebo.

Oh well, that's said. And I'm pretty sure I'm not the only one who was captivated before we came, over the following years, to a fuller understanding of the extent of the cheating.

Twelve years later came the highlight of my 2017 Tour de France. A moment that only few noticed. No cameras or journalists were around or paying attention. After signing on for the last stage of his cycling career, Thomas Voeckler rolled down the podium, in Montgeron, to go and salute his many fans massed behind the barriers. As he was signing autographs, a certain Chris Froome, on his way to a fourth Tour triumph, moved up the ramp to sign and sounds of booing were heard from the crowd. Sounds and shouts that good old Tommy noticed. The Frenchman's face changed. He moved towards the angry fans and told them to shut up, then turned towards the podium where Froome still was, raised his arms in the air and started applauding. That discreet scene – unseen by most – was the highlight of my Tour.

Cycling has changed. Cycling is just as exciting, and I am a privileged man to be able to witness all that . . . in the best possible seat.

For thirteen years now, every morning of every stage of the Tour de France (except for one, due to the unexpectedly early arrival of a little fella), I sit down on the front right seat of Race Direction car number 2. On my left is a man who, in his early years, was considered one of the big hopes of French cycling. *Un sacré moteur* as one would say in French (a hell of an engine). Pascal Lance is his name and many would have said that he could have had the career of another Lance, but let's just say that he decided on a different path. Pascal is totally committed to what he does. A fine driver, he also knows exactly how a rider will react and therefore knows how to anticipate possible problems. I have so much trust in him that I am rarely scared on descents. The problem is that I am now so used to his driving that I tend to fall asleep when zooming down the mountains of the Pyrenees or Alps. A slight problem when you need to be fully focused on the race and riders.

Behind on the left is the Tour de France sporting director, Thierry Gouvenou, a man whom few would have imagined taking over from the mighty Jean-François Pescheux, his predecessor. I now know why Pescheux, the man who taught me everything, or almost, chose Thierry. He knows the race and rules by heart, he knows the roads like his own backyard. I'm astonished by his memory of every single place in France and that is precious when you have to conduct an event like the Tour de France. Consider him as the Herbert von Karajan of La Grande Boucle. And like Pescheux, Gouvenou, despite seeming rather shy and quiet, is pretty scary when he starts yelling at a TV or photographer's motorbike that is not in the right place at the right time.

On Thierry's right is the president of the UCI *commissaires*. Between both of them is one of the most essential items in race direction car number 2: the champagne cooler containing . . . the champagne bottle . . . only to be used in the case of extreme heat (extreme weather protocol does not necessarily apply!).*

The four people in the car therefore remain the same four during the entire Tour and despite how serious we need to be, we share moments of laughter when the race settles down. I can't agree more with one of Christian Prudhomme's favourite quotes: '3000km de sourires' (3000km of smiles). Yes, he's right. And just that makes it worthwhile coming on the Tour.

Being the speaker of Radio Tour is a privilege, yes, but it's also intense work that requires a few assets. Number 1: focus. You have to be fully concentrated on what goes on from kilometre 0 to the finish line. It actually even starts in the neutral zone when a rider might lift his arm for an early puncture or just because he forgot to take a rain jacket (especially in Britain). We are at the service of the actors of this great show so the least we can do is pay attention to what goes on. Also, to be fully focused on what the info motorbikes tell me. Indeed, being sat behind the pack, I can't see what goes on at the front, so I have my 'eyes on the Tour', my three heroes on their big motorbikes, often former pro riders who tell me who is in the breakaway and what the gaps are.

To help me remain fully concentrated, I work with a headset including a mic and a pedal that I press with my foot to speak (pretty helpful when you have a sandwich in one hand and a glass of champagne in the other). It's the kind of device one needs to get used to and adapt to. A few years ago, I turned to my driver to talk to him 'privately' about issues concerning my daily sandwich. I pressed the pedal and told him in a

---

* For your information, extreme heat, hence champagne drinking (one glass and only one), starts at 13.5°C.

frustrated way: '*Pascal, mes cornichons sont au fond de ma sacoche!*' (Pascal, the pickles are at the bottom of my bag), only realising seconds later that I was actually saying that to the entire Tour de France. Naturally SMS messages came flowing in and that ridiculous anecdote was mentioned in *L'Équipe* the following day. It just shows how many people tune in to Radio Tour.

And so to quality number 2: keeping calm. In my first year on the Grande Boucle, a gentleman by the name of Bernard Hinault came up to me at the finish after the third stage. Bernard Hinault, the Badger: a legend, a man I admired and still do. He put his hand on my shoulder and said '*Môme!* [son] You have to keep calm. If you get over-excited, the DSs will get over-excited and that will create chaos. So when there's a crash, say it calmly . . . ' He was right, and I'm not saying that because he is Bernard Hinault and you don't want to mess with the Badger. In moments of drama, when crashes occur, I try to be as clear and precise as possible, give as much information as I possibly can, but I won't yell or shout. *Merci*, Bernard!

Having a good stomach would be the third quality required for the job. The first time I was asked to do Radio Tour was in Qatar on the occasion of what was called, at the time, The Grand-Prix of Doha. It was a bit of a test for me and the people of the organisation (ASO) to see how 'junior' could adapt. The race took place on the Moto GP circuit and several laps were to be covered. In other words: bends, kerbs, turns and more bends . . . I kept it to myself, but after just a few kilometres, I thought I was going to throw up. I guess I've adapted since that day. I did have a slight issue on stage 20 of the 2015 Tour heading to l'Alpe d'Huez.* A bad salami sandwich forced me to jump out of the car going up the Col de la Croix de Fer. *Au revoir*, little red car. Thankfully I found a seat in the *voiture balai* (broom wagon) that graciously drove me back to my initial

---

* Everything that is said here has to remain strictly confidential. What happens in the red car, stays in the red car.

place after a short pause, and I was able to witness the triumph of Thibaut Pinot later that day, after my own triumph on La Croix de Fer.

Finally, sleeping is not a possibility for me ... for obvious reasons mentioned before. When you take on a stage of the Tour de France, like the riders, you need to be fresh. The day will be long, sometimes very long, exhaustingly long. And your eyes will tend to close, slowly, viciously. And that's when you feel a thump on your arm or shoulder and a voice saying: 'Seb, Movistar is calling ... ' or 'Seb, rear wheel puncture for FDJ ... ' Oops. Thankfully, there are four of us in the car and not all four sleep at the same time, especially not the driver ... I hope!

Voilà. My work is my passion. And not many of us are able to live their passion. I have seen things that only a few have witnessed. I have noticed despair, drama, pain, so much pain, some laughter and so many smiles. I have heard insults, yelling, spitting, crying, joking, suffering, so much suffering. I have been scared, worried, flabbergasted, astonished. I have seen champions and villains, but to my eyes, they are all heroes. And to paraphrase what Chris Froome says every year on the finish line of the Tour de France, on the Champs-Elysées: 'I can't wait for the next Tour ... '

10. TOUR DE FRANCE DIARY: WEEK 2

François Thomazeau

Monday, 10 July

Rest day, St Astier

I have the impression I have spent a part of my recent life in the Golden Tulip Hotel in Lyon. It is a non-descript international hotel, rising among a copse of trees between two ring roads in one of those new business zones that have recently cropped up all over France around the stadiums built or refurbished for Euro 2016. The women at the front desk sport the same fabricated smiles as they demand your email; junk mail of promotions and bargains soon pile up in your spam box. The food is presentable yet tasteless, the rooms predictably comfortable – this could be anywhere in Europe or North America. Still, it is a convenient location which I have used often driving back from early season events like Paris–Nice or alpine ski races.

Like most Mondays on the Tour, this is a rest day and it finds you struggling to decide whether you are still in the race or back to normal. Getting up, you are in two minds about putting your accreditation badge around your neck and finally you do not. It is a four-hour drive to Périgueux and the small B&B booked by *The Cycling Podcast* just outside the hamlet of St Astier, in the heart of Dordogne. The trip is rather uneventful as we join holiday travellers in one of those bland motorway services that have become landmarks of life on the Tour. Rain is pouring in buckets as we attempt to leave the steak house in which we had lunch. I make the mistake of ordering tea with milk at the local branch of Paul only to be handed a cardboard cup of a hot foamy white fluid and a teabag. As I bravely plunge the Earl Grey into the cup and stir it, the white liquid slowly turns to beige. I sip on the mixture and realise it does not taste too bad . . . I might have invented a new drink. We'll call it Teapuccino.

Lionel: 'I think I came up with this idea of Teapuccino.'

Richard: 'I beg to differ. It was my idea.'

Who knows? Cycling is an individual sport performed as a team.

The B&B is an isolated ageless mansion half a mile from St Astier village. The landlord is a forthcoming, restless and diminutive figure with a rolled fag on his lip and swears like we are old mates. Wifi connections will be a problem for the rest of the week. I manage to get a signal by leaving the windows and door of my room open. A tweet informs me that the youngest rider in the peloton, Fortuneo's Élie Gesbert, had a far more stressful rest day as he set fire to his room by leaving a towel on a radiator, forcing his hotel to be evacuated. The next day, he would set the race ablaze by breaking away with fellow Frenchman Yoann Offredo.

At aperitif time, we discuss cycling etiquette over beer and pastis as I defend the view that respecting the yellow jersey in the Tour is utter B.S.

Our host is a great cook and treats us to a light and delicious meal of sturgeon. The wine is a treacherous organic Bergerac – Château les Miaudoux – which sends us all to bed when we have a look at the label and discover it was 14.5 degrees.

Tuesday, 11 July

Stage 10: Périgueux–Bergerac, 178km
Stage winner: Marcel Kittel
Yellow jersey: Chris Froome

Back in the saddle for the peloton. Back in my little nest at the back of *The Cycling Podcast* car. Rest days can have strange effects as you ease up and need a fresh shot of adrenalin to keep you going. At the start, I talk to the Madiot brothers, who lost four of their riders in the brave and somewhat stupid attempt to save stage 4 winner Arnaud Démare in the gruelling stage to Chambéry. Française des Jeux manager Marc Madiot and his brother Yvon insist it was worth trying.

'They were already very close but this ordeal really made them even closer now,' Yvon tells me. 'They're more than teammates, they're more than friends. They're like family now.'

And he believes that Démare and his three mates – Mickaël Delage, Jacopo Guarnieri and Ignatas Konovalovas – can become a modern incarnation of the Three Musketeers in future races: 'All for one and one for all'.

The stage is one of the dullest in this Tour. While Gesbert tries to flee as quickly as possible from the scene of his arson, he is joined by maverick compatriot Yoann Offredo, who has already been involved in a doomed two-man move with Taylor Phinney on stage 2. As usual, the two are easily controlled by the likes of Quick-Step's Julien Vermote and Lotto-Soudal's Lars Bak and the peloton crawls back on them in the finale. At the finish, Offredo is furious and he says so, questioning why other teams with no sprinters did not send a rider to join forces with them, to go for a stage win. He suggests that UCI points should be awarded to escapees in order to motivate more riders to try and outwit the sprinters' teams. He even calls on his fellow riders to join him the next morning at the Wanty-Groupe Gobert team bus to make plans for a break the next day on another flat stage to Pau.

It is one of my oddest tasks on this Tour to interview French riders in English for the podcast. Offredo is the star of the day in his home country and he is assailed by a scrum of journalists repeating the same questions over and again. As I step forward to ask for my 'question en anglais', Yoann is ushered back to the finish line where he is to appear on a France Televisions programme. I wait for him as the team buses leave their designated parking areas one by one, leaving but me, a Wanty mechanic and a team car, surrounded by a handful of idle fans begging for caps and *bidons*. Offredo returns some twenty minutes later and obligingly makes his point in English for me.

'It's frustrating. I don't understand why only two teams, Fortuneo and Wanty, go in the break. We are small teams, we need to go in the breaks to have some publicity for our teams. I don't understand why other teams help Quick-Step, because it's always the same guy winning stages. Marcel Kittel is the best sprinter in the world and nobody is trying to stop him. Maybe I'm wrong, maybe it's my first Tour de France and I'm too enthusiastic and naïve. Something's wrong, maybe it's me. Maybe there is not enough motivation for the guys. Why not award points to escapees? Otherwise it's boring for everybody, for spectators following on TV to watch a stage like today.'

He is right. Obviously. And it is a fourth stage win for Kittel, as planned.

Back to our B&B for a delicious meal of filet mignon with mashed parsley buds. We choose a lighter Bergerac wine – Pecharmant – this time.

Wednesday, 12 July

Stage 11: Eymet–Pau, 203.5km
Stage winner: Marcel Kittel
Yellow jersey: Chris Froome

Nobody, it seems, has heard Offredo's call. I bump into him at the start in the lovely little town of Eymet and he finds comfort in the fact that he received several texts of support from his peers. Eymet is your typical south-west town built in a circle around a massive central square with arcades. It is picturesque, lively, clad in Tour colours. It would be a very nice and exciting summer day without the race, which is inevitably going to be as tedious as the previous day. At the Cofidis bus I also ask team manager Yvon Sanquer for his views on the incident

The square in Eymet

that cost his leader Nacer Bouhanni twenty seconds and two hundred Swiss francs for punching Jack Bauer in a brawl shortly before the sprint in Pau. Videos on Twitter show the New Zealander elbowing the Frenchman, who reacts by shoving him aside. Without much action in the race, it is the talk of the morning, everyone claiming to hold a truth that seems to depend mostly on national prejudices.

Marcel Kittel wins his fifth stage with his usual class and ease. What to say? The green jersey seems to cling firmly to his large back. Never trust Tour de France certitudes.

At the finish in Pau, I rush to the technical zone and to the bus sheltering TV and radio commentators to interview Jean-François Bernard about 20 July 1987, the day his career took a definitive turn for the worse.

'You're sure you don't want to talk about something else?' asks 'Jeff', who obviously retains bitter memories of that fateful day.

Bernard was in the yellow jersey at the start of a stage to Villard-de-Lans but his bratty, arrogant attitude angered his rivals, who decided to join forces to make him lose the Tour. Stephen Roche's Carrera and Charly Mottet's Système-U made plans to ambush the Frenchman at the day's feed zone, set in narrow, tricky, winding roads. False race *soigneurs* holding dummy musettes were enough to halt Bernard, who had punctured just before the designated spot. He finished the stage two minutes down and had to settle for third in Paris. The great hopeful of French cycling would never have a second chance.

'It could have changed my life,' he still regrets now.

After the interview, we head for the press room, set as usual in the luxurious Palais Beaumont, a congress hall located next to a casino in a large park in the centre of Pau. The venue has earned cult status among journalists as the place where the media bunch learnt in 2007 – in the middle of a David Millar press conference – that Alexander Vinokourov had failed a dope test for a blood transfusion. The Kazakh was later quoted as saying: 'If I received a blood transfusion from my father, as has been reported, I would have failed a dope test for vodka.'

Pau is part of the Tour history as the second most visited town by the race after Paris and it brings back countless memories of my twenty-seven previous editions – singing Police songs until three in the morning in a bar as a young Tour rookie in 1987, a gloomy press room in 1994 one day after the death of Fabio Casartelli. Palais Beaumont is also the place where Richard Moore interviewed me about my experience of the 1986 Tour for his book *Slaying the Badger*. A first encounter leading to a friendship that would later take me on board *The Cycling Podcast*.

The old Pau magic seems to work again as Richard and I inadvertently meet Stephen Roche as we are leaving the press centre. The 1987 winner tells us his own version of the 1987 destruction of Jeff Bernard.

'It's not the story as I remember it, it's the story as it was,' he insists.

And against Bernard's claims that he had lost the Tour that day, the Irishman replies: 'Where were you in Morzine, Jeff? Where were you in La Plagne?'

Same player shoots again. And scores.

Thursday, 13 July

Stage 12: Pau–Peyragudes, 214.5km
Stage winner: Romain Bardet
Yellow jersey: Fabio Aru

It seems to be raining every time we leave Pau. The start area is lined along the panoramic Boulevard des Pyrenees but this year there is no panorama to enjoy because of the mist. FDJ sports director Yvon Madiot tells me Thibaut Pinot, third in the 2014 Tour, will attack today. He does but only spends a dozen minutes in the front before being reeled in. The French climber has left too much energy in his narrowly unsuccessful quest for the Giro podium and he is not really in contention. He will later call it quits and pledge not to ride two successive Grand Tours ever again.

At the AG2R bus, former pro-turned-DS Stéphane Goubert is looking after French prospect Pierre Latour, then in contention for the best young rider jersey. Latour is a climber well-suited to the Pyrenees, Goubert tells me. I wonder what the difference is with the Alps.

'I don't know,' he replies. 'But they're different. You can feel instinctively they're not the same. Maybe it's greener here, the climbs are softer, the landscape less aggressive. It's a different feel, a different scent, a different philosophy. I like the Pyrenees best,' says Goubert, who rode ten Tours and six Vueltas.

The road to Peyragudes is a long one and when we finally reach the Peyresourde pass and the finish area, a race steward stops us and orders that we park some two kilometres away from the press centre, at the foot of the final climb. The sun strikes hard and we can spot the media tent on a hillside in the distance. I decide to walk up the gruelling final 500 metres, at a gradient of 17 per cent. I only have my bag hanging from my right shoulder but I find the short walk daunting. I can hardly breathe when I cross the finish line to the caustic grin of another race warden. In three hours' time, the best riders in the world will tackle the same ascent on their bikes. Good luck to them.

Waiting for the race to unfold, I try to overcome my fear of heights by standing on the edge of a ravine to answer questions about retiring French legend Thomas Voeckler for InCycle TV. My interviewer is gifted. She also persuades me to stick my tongue out à la Voeckler.

Back in the press tent, my colleagues wake up from a snooze, the side-effect of a tasty buffet of salmon and black pudding, when Contador launches one of his several short-lived attacks in this Tour de France. I

Missing, presumed stolen. Black pudding

just created a diplomatic incident inside *The Cycling Podcast* team by nicking a slice of black pudding off Lionel's plate. We shall overcome.

The stage finale is one of the most exciting in this Tour. New Zealand's George Bennett attacks from the foot but quickly hits a wall, while Chris Froome starts to struggle. His teammate Mikel Landa looks the freshest of the lot and while we'll never know what the Spaniard said to sports director Nicolas Portal on the radio, the two exchange strong words in Spanish on the line. Meanwhile France's favourite son Romain Bardet has surged to snatch an exciting victory. At his jubilant AG2R bus, Stéphane Goubert responds to my questions with the only English sentence he knows: 'I love you.' He looks so proud and elated that it is probably true. At the Team Sky bus, Froome can hardly hide his disappointment. Clearly hampered by hunger knock in the last stretch, he replies to our questions more diplomatically than ever: 'I just didn't have the legs,' he repeats.

Dusk is crawling over Peyragudes when we hurry back to the car in the fog, from which emerges a strange vehicle: a yellow 2CV sporting a James Bond 007 logo. The small Pyrenees resort is the spot where the opening scene of *Tomorrow Never Dies* was shot.

Down in the valley, in Bagnères-de-Luchon, where I joined my first Tour de France in 1986, we treat ourselves to a simple but substantial meal of local specialties. Frog legs are on the menu.

Chris Froome didn't have the legs. I did. With a bottle of Madiran.

Friday 14 July

Stage 13: St Girons–Foix, 101km
Stage winner: Warren Barguil
Yellow jersey: Fabio Aru

This is one of those stages when we decide to skip the start. I'm a quote provider for the official website of Tour organisers ASO but a few phone calls to sports directors and press officers has me covered. The road to Foix brings a strange impression of déjà-vu. I almost certainly drove these roads before. Our stomachs rejoice when the massive château de Foix appears as we gear up for one of the most anticipated press buffets of the Tour. The press centre is another sports hall but it has been built by the river Ariège and that is where our lunch of local delicatessen is served. We are handed enormous amounts of pâté, saucisson and sausage, and we sit by the stream, looking on, as canoeists slalom around poles. There is a relaxed garden party atmosphere to it all. I had too much to eat – as is often the case when we reach the south-west – and as I make it back to the heat of the press centre, I think of a great headline should Froome struggle again: Chris de Foix.

A crisis there is as Contador has attacked again in the company of compatriot and Froome teammate Landa, who at one stage comes dangerously close to the yellow jersey. After the Peyragudes incident, everybody is now wondering about Landa's loyalty to his leader. Both will later insist that the Team Sky gameplan is as bright as the Ariège water and that Landa is paid to know where he stands. Still rumours abound about his transfer next season: Movistar seemed to be front of the queue, but now some insist the partnership with Contador in the day's break was a foretaste of their future collaboration with Trek-Segafredo. Astana sports director Dmitry Fofonov tells me the next day that Landa – who rode for the Kazakh team two seasons before – has renewed his contract with Sky. Bunch gossip.

Meanwhile, Warren Barguil and Nairo Quintana have caught the two Spaniards and the Frenchman ultimately outsprints the lot in Foix. The castle resembles the Bastille before its destruction in 1789. A French victory on Bastille Day is always a special moment for the fans. It is even more special as Warren Barguil, the polka-dot jersey on his back, revives memories of former crowd favourites Richard Virenque and even Bernard Hinault. There is a hint of controversy as he claims to have double nationality as a Frenchman and a Breton. It is all quickly forgotten as his child-like smile, natural good humour and sheer class spur an instant wave of Barguil mania. Twitter finds a tag for it: #wawapowa.

After the stage, I am pressed to sing *La Marseillaise* on the podcast and I do, much to the surprise of a *L'Équipe* driver sitting nearby and thus far unaware of my musical skills.

I am then interviewed by Australian colleague and friend Rob Arnold, founder of *Ride* magazine, about why the French do not call their national day Bastille Day. I have no idea but it is a fact. For us it is simply *Le 14 juillet*.

We are staying in a hotel which I'd stayed in before and I take magret de canard at a restaurant where I had it before. Richard and Lionel are brave enough to go for cassoulet. Our colleagues David Walsh, Rupert Guinness and Gregor Brown narrowly missed the time cut. It will be Chinese food for them tonight. We have a bottle of organic Faugères too many.

Saturday, 15 July

Stage 14: Blagnac–Rodez, 181.5km
Stage winner: Michael Matthews
Yellow jersey: Chris Froome

Blagnac is also a familiar fixture on the Tour map. It is the home of the Toulouse aeronautic industry, the site of its airport and I recall days when the bunch started from the tarmac, amid replicas – or were they genuine? – of Concorde and the space shuttle Columbia. It might have been 1990 and an ominous stage win by Miguel Indurain in Luz-Ardiden. We are headed for Rodez so it is normal to talk to Greg Van Avermaet at the podium. I find this man so humble and underrated, staying as he does quietly in the shadow of Peter Sagan despite boasting a comparable – if not better – record. The Olympic champion and Paris–Roubaix winner answers remarkably in three languages and tells us how much his stage win in Rodez two years ago meant to him.

'Rodez was a special moment in my career. Before that win, I had high expectations, I was always close. But Rodez made a big change in my life. It was the launch pad for other big victories. I'm happy the Tour de France put it in again.'

I also talk to Michael Matthews at the Team Sunweb bus where he goes almost unnoticed amidst the Wawa craze. Since joining the German-Dutch outfit this season, Bling* is a little less chatty, more focused. And it pays off as the next few hours will show.

'The legs are good. It's been nice so far. I did not waste too much energy doing silly things. The Tour has not been so hard,' he claims.

Many would disagree, but the Australian had it so tough in the past on the Grande Boucle that it is easy to understand what he means. Matthews is another exciting rider of a new species including the likes of Sagan, Van Avermaet or Michal Kwiatkowski. A versatile rider who can sprint and climb pretty well. A world title – he came close two years ago – and a major classic are all he needs to stand on par with the aforementioned Belgian. His two stage wins on this Tour and his green jersey are more than a good start.

In Rodez, he times his move perfectly, outwits Van Avermaet and Edvald Boasson Hagen and makes it two in succession for Team Sunweb. Lovers of meaningless stats ask around when last did two room-mates win back-to-back Tour stages. God only knows. But the result is certainly a great reward for a team that has done a lot to renew the image of cycling since its early days as Skil-Shimano. A bunch of nice, dedicated and friendly riders who made it all the way to the top together in the slipstream of Giro champion Tom Dumoulin.

'We have great fun,' says Matthews, which sums it up nicely.

* Yellow card, François, for 'Bling'.

At the finish, I simply cannot get to the line as it means walking over a panoramic viaduct overlooking the valley. I make a brave effort but give up. My fear of heights is stronger than my commitment to the cause.

I must confess that the highlight of the day is dinner. I booked a table at Rodez one-star restaurant Goûts et Couleurs, where I've been fortunate enough to eat twice before. It has improved again as we sit in the summer patio with Associated Press and Reuters colleagues alongside Tour de France press chief and gourmet Philippe Sudres. Unfortunately, Lionel is listed as DNS, having had too much of the local speciality *aligot* – mashed potatoes with Cantal cheese – for lunch. Goûts et Couleurs (Tastes and Colours) is aptly named as the chef is also a painter and his plates are as tasty to look at as they are colourful to the palate. I go for the house classic Calamars à la Soulages, a remarkable culinary homage to Rodez-born painter Pierre Soulages, whose museum attracts more than 400,000 visitors in town annually. By far my best meal of the Tour and a great wine discovery – Valérie Guérin's Fitou.

Sunday, 16 July

Stage 15: Laissac-Severac–Le Puy-en-Velay, 189.5km
Stage winner: Bauke Mollema
Yellow jersey: Chris Froome

We are often asked what we do at the start of stages and why we talk to riders about topics that will be outdated a few hours later. It is at the start that you often grab the better stories, the ones with insight and perspective.

At the foot of the podium, I spot Belgium's Tim Wellens, one of the most promising riders of his generation. He is an elegant well-mannered young man and a huge talent, whom I saw win the Montreal Grand

Prix two years ago. He had been in a very bad way the previous day and I ask him about the rumour that he has refused a therapeutic use exemption (TUE) to improve his condition.

'When it's very hot, I have allergies on my legs. This year, it's very strong. Maybe with a TUE, it could have been better but we decided it was better not to do it in competition. I hope it will get better,' he tells me.

A few hours later, he unfortunately calls it quits.

We have done three-quarters of the Tour and the toll is high on the bodies. Yoann Offredo also arrives at the podium and he greets me as he collects bottles and food supplements supplied at the start by the organisers. He is no longer an angry man, no longer the maverick enthusiastic Tour de France rookie he was two weeks ago. He is just depressed.

'I was far from realising that the Tour de France is a great show, with a huge amount of people around you, with a lot of crowds, a lot of staff, a lot of journalists but that in the end it left you all alone in front of your doubts. When you go to bed at night and pick the roadbook and ask yourself: will I be able to make it? It's something I'm struggling with,' he tells me.

The previous day, he was spotted by Radio Tour speaker Seb Piquet in tears on the finish line. Offredo will finally complete his first Tour de France at thirty years of age. A great personal victory.

We decide to drive the course for once and it is the right decision as the route is simply smashing. The Aubrac plateau is home to one of the best breed of cows in the country and they are looking at us from a distance, scattered along the green bumps known as puys in the region. The stage is one of the welcome additions to the itinerary decided by Tour designer Thierry Gouvenou and it includes spectacular climbs like the Peyra Taillade ascent close to the finish. Picturesque châteaux complete the scenery of a stage vaguely reminiscent of previous days. Chris Froome suffers a mechanical and he finally returns to the bunch with the help of his teammates, including a somewhat reluctant Mikel Landa. At the finish line, Dave Brailsford insists the soon-to-be four

Yoann Offredo, Pédaleur de Charme

times Tour champion is stronger than ever. 'Some say he showed signs of weakness but the way he made it back to the bunch is in my opinion rather a show of strength,' he tells me.

The stage win goes to Bauke Mollema, who is slowly turning into a winner after renouncing his GC ambitions. This is another trend of this Tour as we have seen several would-be GC contenders settling for stage wins like Barguil or Mollema and it accounts for a more exciting race.

While the team buses leave the finish area one after the other, the AG2R bus is stuck. This is Romain Bardet's home region and the fans are flocking around the coach, determined not to leave before they catch a glimpse of their hero.

We are staying in a little town some thirty kilometres outside of Le Puy, close to the next day's course. The hotel has seen better days. Or maybe not.

11. FRENCH JINX

François Thomazeau

On 16 July 1986, I embarked on my first Tour de France. Embarked is the right word. I did not have a clue, I did not have a car, I had no hotels, no accreditation. No fear either. I had only joined Reuters for a couple of weeks when rival news agency Agence France Presse went on strike. Typically. Reuters decided we had to beef up our Tour coverage and off I went. Took a plane to Pau, a cab to Luchon. I made it to the press room late in the afternoon and was greeted at the *Permanence* desk by a young man named Philippe Sudres, who was the son of the Tour press chief. Philippe looked at my only credential – a written letter from my news editor – pondered my case and decided to give me a 'technician' badge. Little did we know at the time that we would still be close friends thirty years later. And little did we suspect that these three decades would go by without another French winner of the Tour de France.

My Tour debut was an ominous one. I was on the plane and then on the road when Bernard Hinault staged one of the most enigmatic moves of his entire career. A solid yellow jersey holder, with a 5:25 lead over his theoretical team leader Greg LeMond, the Badger attacked on the Tourmalet descent and went solo, only to crack on the climb to Superbagnères and squander 4:39 to the American to retain a slim 40-second margin over him on the line. The rest is history as LeMond would go on to win this sensational 1986 edition while France would keep waiting in vain for a successor to Hinault, who had clinched his fifth Tour title a year earlier.

I had reached Luchon too late to write about the Superbagnères stage. I would have to wait for the next stage to Blagnac to deliver my first Tour story. As far as I remember, it was not very good. Neither was my baptism of fire. Seeing the other reporters rush away from the press centre when the peloton came within 10 km of the finish line, I was not too sure what to do. As an agency man, I had to wait for the stage to finish to send my story as quickly as I could. I then hurried to the line, which was actually only metres away from my position. I ran down a small mound, jumped over a ditch . . . and found myself face to face with a cyclist coming my way, a yellow jersey on his back. An angry grin was running across his face. I was at a loss what to do so I ran after him shouting: 'Bernard! Bernard!' As I drew close he just shoved me aside without a word. That was my first ever encounter with a pro rider.

Never since has a French rider seemed so poised to win the Tour again – not even Laurent Fignon in 1989, when he lost to the same LeMond by eight seconds – and I sometimes like to believe I might be responsible for the jinx. Another strange thing happened to me in that 1989 edition – on the TGV taking the peloton and a few journalists all the way back to Paris for the final time trial, all my colleagues were besieging the car in which Fignon, the obvious winner in everybody's view, was sitting. There was an empty seat next to LeMond and I found myself sitting there, listening for nearly two hours to the American's tale of his 1986 Tour triumph, his hunting accident and his incredible return to form. I did not take any notes. I did not record our chat. All my stories were ready for another Tour win by France's Fignon. We know what happened next.

The day I quit, one of my fellow men will probably bridge this lingering gap. In the meantime, I am left to try and find out why and how it happened.

Multifactorial is a trendy word. Not sure it existed back in 1986. But there are many reasons for the French failure to win the Tour for so long. All of them extremely different. That the drought started in 1986 is certainly not an accident. LeMond's victory was the first step in the globalisation of cycling that would continue and expand in the following years. In 1987, Stephen Roche became the first Irishman to win the race. English was more widespread in the peloton, even though both LeMond and Roche had to make their apprenticeship in France, the traditional homeland of road cycling. Two years before, Colombians had made their first impression on the Tour when Luis Herrera won at l'Alpe d'Huez. There were twenty-six of them at the start of the 1986 Tour! And nine Americans, two Canadians, one New Zealander, one Australian and a Yugoslav. Cycling was no longer confined to its traditional playground of western continental Europe. Other cycling powers did not fare any better since then. For while the French have not won the Tour since 1985, the Dutch have not done so since 1980 and the Belgians since 1976!

It was precisely the thought at the basis of Dave Brailsford's foundation of Team Sky that road cycling was still a rather small and secretive sport in the early noughties, leaving plenty of room for innovation and improvement. The interest generated by LeMond's Tour victory in the US, followed by the collapse of the Eastern Bloc and the massive arrival of talent from former communist countries would change the face of the sport for ever. The competition was simply becoming much stronger and varied, making it more difficult for a nation to dominate the sport, even though Belgium kept the upper hand in the classics and Spain in the Grand Tours.

The second factor is probably generational. It is not simple to breed exceptional talents like Jacques Anquetil, Louison Bobet, Bernard Hinault or Laurent Fignon and there is often a backlash in a sporting nation after such overwhelming personalities retire. More importantly, cycling had moved completely out of fashion when Bernard Tapie poured big money into the sport in 1984 to try and revive its image and success. Even so, Tapie's other sport venture as the owner of Olympique Marseille from 1986 to his infamous downfall seven years later, was far more popular as Marseille became European champions in 1993. For the French youth of the time, cycling was an old-fashioned sport surviving mainly in some rural pockets of la France profonde like Brittany or the south-west, and urban riders like Fignon or Eric Boyer were rare exceptions to the rule. While cycling was becoming a trendy, rather posh discipline in the English-speaking world, French youngsters were dreaming of Michel Platini, Zinedine Zidane or of the much more exciting world of the NBA and Michael Jordan. And if they bought a bicycle, it was a mountain bike.

Of course, there were still plenty of excellent French riders in the peloton between 1986 and the Festina scandal in 1998, but Richard Virenque, Laurent Jalabert, Christophe Moreau or Luc Leblanc were potential Tour winners in their own minds only.

The third problem was that the globalisation of cycling had a regrettable tendency to mix the best of the new world – technical innovations, training techniques – with the worst of the old – namely doping and corruption. Habits die hard and it took a long time for century-old traditions to collapse. And the first step of this mutation of cycling was undoubtedly Festina. As a pioneer sport in terms of doping, cycling was the first hit when the police took over from sport authorities to tackle the problem. And France, as the homeland of cycling, was also the first to be caught when the gendarmes started raiding the Tour de France. It has become an urban legend in France to claim that local riders stopped performing well from 1998 because they had stopped taking drugs while the others were still on them. But it is not entirely wrong, as facts later confirmed. Festina did not really harm cycling. It harmed French cycling. The return of Lance Armstrong in 1999 was deemed the start of a new era. We know what to think about it now. And Italy did not really care about doping until the *carabinieri* blitzed the Giro in 2001. The Germans were not seriously concerned about performance-enhancing drugs in cycling before the Telekom case in 2007. The Danes could not care less about the problem until Bjarne Riis confessed the same year. The Dutch had to wait for the once invincible Rabobank team to fall apart to realise they had nursed a generation of dopers. Spanish riders kept winning effortlessly until Operación Puerto in 2006 cast doubts on some of their performances. And Americans kept believing in miracles until 2012 and Armstrong's coming out.

In fact,1998 was a considerable trauma for French cycling. Its key players, taken to the police station, sometimes detained or charged, were in a state of shock. As the now deceased former Renault–Elf rider Pierre-Henri Menthéour put it: 'We, the half-gods, were treated like criminals.' It was a shattering wake-up call, especially as the Festina team of Virenque,

Moreau, Laurent Brochard, Pascal Hervé or Didier Rous looked almost unbeatable. Richard Virenque told me in a recent interview he was convinced he would have won the Tour without the Festina scandal. 'We were flying,' he said.

The scandal was a dreadful crash-landing and then the Armstrong era started. As a cancer survivor, he was untouchable. It was easy for him to bully French riders and claim they were pussies who simply did not train hard enough, which was not necessarily entirely wrong. For what was left of the French peloton, the heart was simply not in it any more. The best riders of that generation had been with Festina or in the case of Jalabert with Manolo Saiz. A low profile was preferable. As for the teams themselves, they had to change their attitude radically. Team managers Marc Madiot or Roger Legeay spent some time in custody while Vincent Lavenu had to start all over again after his Casino team was also hit by the EPO scandal. For all of them, it was a life-changing experience and the teams they started after 1998 – like Jean-René Bernaudeau's Bonjour – embraced a whole new philosophy leading to the creation of the MPCC (Mouvement Pour un Cyclisme Crédible). It took nearly fifteen years for this reconstruction scheme to take place.

Another key date to understand France's woes is 1990. That year, LeMond won his third and last Tour. For many it was EPO's year zero. Cycling would never be the same again. The doping arsenal had now reached a point at which any average rider could prevail, if he was bold enough to take the right stuff, tough enough to deny it and corrupt enough to respect the *omertà*. 1990 was also the year of the birth of Thibaut Pinot, Romain Bardet and Nacer Bouhanni. Warren Barguil and Arnaud Démare were born a year later. All those young men were small-town boys, coming from the traditional strongholds of French cycling, Brittany, Auvergne, Picardie, the Vosges Region. But they took up cycling with a brand-new approach, inspired by the modernity of the world around them. Their idols were no longer Anquetil, Bobet, Poulidor or Hinault, names they might hardly ever have heard of. They had their own cycling history to write. A post-Armstrong, post-EPO history.

Now, more than thirty years after the last victory of a Frenchman in the Tour de France, the country has never had such a wide range of cycling potential with three riders finishing on the Tour podium in four years – Jean-Christophe Péraud and Thibaut Pinot in 2014, Romain Bardet in 2016 and 2017 – while Warren Barguil clinched the KOM title in 2017 and might become a serious GC contender in the next few seasons. With Démare, Bouhanni and Bryan Coquard, the French also have gifted sprinters who can target some of the most prestigious classics in the cycling calendar. And better is still to come we are told with FDJ's David Gaudu, the winner of the 2016 Tour de l'Avenir, described as the rider with 'the biggest engine' of the new generation. Gaudu was born in 1996.

It is about time I retire.

12. TOUR DE FRANCE DIARY: WEEK 3

Lionel Birnie

Monday, 17 July

Rest day, Mazet-Saint-Voy

No chance of a rest day lie-in at the Auberge du Soleil in Mazet-Saint-Voy thanks to a light breeze which made the wooden shutters over my window rattle all night. A folded-up copy of *L'Équipe* wedged in the gap worked for a while but the wind won in the end, as it always does, and from six onwards I lie with the sausage-shaped pillow over my head. It's my fourth sausage-shaped pillow of the Tour. Why, France? Why persist with the sausage-shaped pillow in the twenty-first century?

Just before eight, I admit defeat and go down to breakfast, only to find an *echapée* of flies feasting in rotation on the croissants and bread lying in the basket on the breakfast table. Things like this send my morale plummeting, although I always try to remember that the riders sometimes don't have things much better. A couple of years ago, Team Sky and AG2R spent their rest day in a chain hotel sandwiched between the autoroute and an industrial abattoir near Sisteron. The hum of the motorway and a livery smell hung in the air and the hotel's foyer and restaurant was full of flies.

Unlike the riders, at least we don't usually have to share rooms, except in extreme situations. There was the time our travelling companion Tom Cary of the *Telegraph* booked what he thought would be a triple room but which turned out to be a family room with a double bed and a single bunk above it. For a while it looked like Tom and Richard would have to share the double like Daddy Bear and Mummy Bear, with me clambering up the ladder to sleep above them. Fortunately, Monsieur managed to find me a fold-up bed, although I was sure he dragged out the search for longer than necessary just to make us panic a bit. So, although the Auberge du Soleil is less than sunny, it could be worse.

Simon is back, refreshed, after a family holiday in Portugal. I'm not sure what he finds more challenging – dealing with the wants and needs of three young children or the wants and needs of three podcasters – and I'm not sure I want to ask. (To be fair, François is very low maintenance.)

Simon has plotted a 30-kilometre bike ride taking us into the countryside. The roads are quiet, the scenery is stunning and although it turns out to be the final time I ride my bike during the Tour, it leaves me feeling ready for the final week.

In the afternoon, we drive over to Le Puy-en-Velay to meet Louis Meintjes of UAE-Team Emirates. Meintjes is lying eighth overall, best of the rest, really, and it's fair to say he's staking a claim to succeed Haimar Zubeldia as the rider most adept at forcing his way into the lower reaches of the top ten without anyone actually noticing him. It doesn't turn out to be the most scintillating interview but perhaps we are guilty of expecting all the riders to be able to articulate the experience of racing in the Tour. I ask him what it's like to be just hanging on when the pace in the mountains stays high for kilometre after kilometre. It's the sort of question that might sometimes elicit an interesting, expansive response but on this occasion it just makes me sound a bit daft. The unspoken answer is, 'It's bloody hard work.'

Back at the auberge, Richard, François and I convene for a pre-prandial drink and to record an episode of *Kilometre 0* about music that has been inspired by the Tour. Music is François's great passion and so we navigate our way through an episode that just about manages to avoid infringing the intellectual properties of the BBC's *Desert Island Discs* and *Juke Box Jury*.

We listen to the songs on my laptop. Most of them are absolutely dreadful, especially a cover of the great Kraftwerk song 'Tour de France' by former Danish rider Jesper Skibby. Famously, Skibby's bike was run over by the chief *commissaire*'s car on the Koppenberg during the 1987 Tour of Flanders. I feel all copies of his record should have gone the same way. Jean-François Bernard's 1988 'hit' is equally awful, and perhaps solely responsible for his failure to follow up his third place in the Tour the previous year. However, it does make me wonder what it would take to get Romain Bardet in the studio.

The exceptions include the catchy 'Bon Dieu, Où Est Ce Peloton', the 1969 smash by Les Frères Jacques (it's as if Led Zeppelin, the Beatles, and the Who didn't even happen in France), and 'Le Coureur' by Sauveur Merlan, which just happens to be the *nom de plume* of François Thomazeau. One day, we'll get him to sing it on the podcast.

Finally, it's time for dinner and the auberge redeems itself with a surprisingly nice pork cheek stew and rice.

Tuesday, 18 July

Stage 16: Le Puy-en-Velay–Romans-sur-Isère, 165km
Stage winner: Michael Matthews
Yellow jersey: Chris Froome

I can't get 'Où Est Ce Peloton' out of my head this morning. The peloton is in Le Puy-en-Velay but we're unlikely to see them in a hurry because we have realised too late that the most direct route to the start would take us the wrong way along the race route. That is a no-no once the publicity caravan has set off, as it is about to. The alternative is a long cross-country detour so we decide to cut our losses, skip the start and head straight to Romans-sur-Isère. Rest-day complacency has set in and it's a reminder to regain our focus and check the roadbook the night before.

On our way, we hear that Marcel Kittel has been dropped on an early climb and for the first time in the Tour his grip on the green jersey weakens. Later on, there's excitable chatter about potential crosswinds, but my attention is briefly diverted by the buffet at the press room and the abundance of local apricots. I find myself eating four or five apricots in quick succession and spend the afternoon wondering if I've overdosed on vitamins, such is the shock to my system, which is now 43 per cent cheese.

The finish line is a good two or three kilometres from the press room. Richard sets off on his Brompton, François and I get in the car. On our way, we pass a French journalist who has misjudged the distance and has broken into a run. We do the decent thing and offer him a lift the rest of the way, dumping the car and walking the remaining few hundred metres. The sun is so strong, I duck from one side of the road to the other, chasing the shade, then remember I have my baseball hat, a gift from one of the podcast's past sponsors, Trainer Road, in my bag. Richard later tells me he thinks it makes me look like an American football coach, which I don't think is a compliment, although it's an improvement on Radish Head, which he called me when he was under the influence of strong painkillers (taken to treat his bad hip) when I caught the sun earlier in the Tour.

Michael Matthews wins the stage and as the riders come to a halt near me I witness the minor argy-bargy between him and John Degenkolb, who felt the Australian had taken liberties in the sprint. Matthews responds by whooping loudly to the sky and Degenkolb pedals off.

I decide to join the queue to speak to the Belgian champion Oliver Naesen, who had done a great deal of work to keep Romain Bardet safe in the crosswinds. A few journalists ask him questions in Flemish and French and just as it's my turn a man I can only call Irritating Belgian Radio Man butts in. It's not the first time Irritating Belgian Radio Man has done this to me and so I say, 'I was next,' fully aware of how pathetic this sounds. 'We're live,' he replies. Naesen shrugs and says, 'They're live,' as if that explains everything. It's at moments like this that the whole exercise seems faintly absurd. Here's a man who's just raced his bike hard for almost four hours, a film of sweat covers his face and body leaving white salt marks on his skin. His chest still heaves up and down as his lungs try to recover from the effort. And two grown men are competing to ask him questions all about it. And I'm one of those men. It's enough to bring on an existential crisis.

On our way back, we offer a lift to a German journalist whose post-race interview etiquette is even worse than Irritating Belgian Radio Man's. He gets in, realises we're going to be stuck in a traffic jam and decides to get out and walk.

'He's very German, that guy,' says François. I don't agree with lazy national stereotyping but in this case I know exactly what he means.

Dinner with a view in Romans-sur-Isère

Dinner in the evening is restorative. Delicious delicate fish accompanied by cold white wine on the terrace overlooking the river.

Wednesday, 19 July

Stage 17: La Mure–Serre Chevalier, 183km
Stage winner: Primoz Roglic
Yellow jersey: Chris Froome

Richard is off to spend the day in the Cannondale-Drapac team car with their sports director Ken Vanmarcke, who is the brother of their cobbled Classics specialist, Sep.

'Don't forget to go to the toilet before you set off,' I say to Richard, remembering an awkward day I'd had in a team car at the Dauphiné once when I thought I wasn't going to be able to hold on long enough and I wasn't brave enough to ask the sports director to stop.

There's an edgy atmosphere around the Cannondale-Drapac team bus, partly because Rigoberto Urán is lying in second place overall and on the verge of a career-defining result, and partly because the boss Jonathan Vaughters has turned up.

'They're keeping me away from Rigo so he doesn't pick up on my nerves,' says Vaughters, almost hopping from foot to foot. 'In fact, they're keeping me away from all the riders today.'

Richard's day out means François can escape his nest and ride in the front like a grown-up. As the crow flies it's only about forty-five kilometres from La Mure to Serre Chevalier but there's no road to take us the shortest way. The riders are taking a northern route, crossing the Col de la Croix de Fer, the Col du Télégraphe and the Col du Galibier, which at 2,645 metres is the highest point of this year's Tour. We're taking the southern route, covering almost two hundred kilometres on busy, single-carriageway roads.

François doesn't drive. It's not that he can't, but after years living in

Paris and Marseille he has no need for a car and I have to concede that the Tour de France is not the place to do your only driving of the year. Ordinarily it would annoy me to have a non-driving companion at the Tour but it's impossible to be annoyed with François, because he's such interesting company. I put on the BBC's *Desert Island Discs* featuring John McEnroe and François spends the next half an hour telling me entertaining stories about his time working for the press office at the Roland Garros tennis tournament. Later on, we pass a field that he tells me hosted the French junior cross-country championships he took part in (or something like that). He wears his multiple talents so lightly I'm bracing myself for the revelation that he wrote all the songs on *Revolver* (or enter your own favourite Beatles album here).

I give him cause to be annoyed with me, though, by stopping for a coffee in Corps and allowing half of the slow-moving team buses to go past. As ever, he's good enough not to show any irritation. We have to wait ages before a rare bit of dual carriageway enables us to move half a dozen places back up the GC.

On reaching Serre-Chevalier we find a bar and watch the race on television before crossing the street just in time for the riders to arrive back at their team buses. I speak to LottoNL-Jumbo's sports director, Nico Verhoeven, who explains that the stage winner, Primoz Roglic, had spent some time training at Serre-Chevalier earlier in the year and had specifically targeted this day. They make it sound so easy when everything works out but I wonder how many other riders had specifically targeted today?

Richard re-joins us and we are then ambushed somewhat by Ned Boulting and David Millar who, in the spirit of friendly generosity, seem to order beers for twice the number of people that are round our table. It seems ungrateful not to help finish them off. Our podcast recording is slightly boisterous as a result, and the beer may have been responsible for Richard saving all the audio files in the wrong format and leaving me to redo them while he and François headed off to dinner, I couldn't say for sure.

Thursday, 20 July

Stage 18: Briançon–Col d'Izoard, 179.5km
Stage winner: Warren Barguil
Yellow jersey: Chris Froome

The plan is to set off early so we reach the top of the Col d'Izoard
before the women's race, La Course, even leaves Briançon. Simon heads
to the supermarket to buy some ham, cheese, fruit and maybe a bar of
chocolate each to keep us going. Richard is annoyed because it's already
eight minutes past the time we agreed was our latest departure time, so
I call Simon and tell him to come back, even though he's already in the
ham and cheese aisle. Richard then realises he's left his wallet up in his
room. It turns out his wallet was in his bag all along and in the time
it's taken for Walletgate to resolve itself, I calculate that Simon could
have bought a week's worth of provisions at the supermarket.

The idea of spending all day on the mountain with nothing to eat
has me at my most Eeyore-ish. 'It'll be fine,' I say. 'I think there's a
supermarket at the top of the Izoard.'

No one laughs.

I should have waited until we'd picked up Orla. She'd have laughed.

Halfway up the mountain we see a bar-café set back from the road.
Orla goes off to investigate. To my eyes the place is shimmering slightly
with the promise of croissants and coffee. Unfortunately, all that's
available is what's left after what appears to have been a human tornado
has swept through the breakfast buffet. It occurs to me that we're doing
the equivalent of minesweeping, the act of going round a pub drinking
the dregs from all the abandoned glasses (although I must stress I am
not speaking from experience here). I cut the end off a piece of bread
that looks suspiciously like it has a bite mark in it and grab the last
banana before anyone else sees it.

We arrive at the top of the Izoard. It's one of those days when we

Lionel, Richard and Orla on the Col d'Izoard

record the podcast in bits as the action unfolds. We've got a few episodes on the go – we're making our normal Tour de France stage show, an episode of *The Cycling Podcast Féminin* focusing on La Course, plus an experimental, free-form episode called 'The Road Trip', which already contains material I think it might be unwise to broadcast.

Richard and Orla summon me over. They're already laughing, I assume at my expense. The red light is already on Richard's recorder.

'What's the Sex Shop Time Trial?' asks Orla.

I feel my face go the colour of the lanterne rouge.

It's all very innocent, I explain. Simon and I grew up a couple of doors away from each other and it's fair to say I more or less forced him to take an interest in cycling. I was a little Henri Desgrange, organising stage races, drawing elaborate routes and profiles in a big notebook, enforcing the rules with a little too much zeal, and making my own leaders' jerseys. Simon was persuaded to take part in my calendar of classics and stage races. One of our regular race routes went from one village to another, turning left at the mysterious shop of adult interest. However, I had no idea, until very recently, that Simon had named it the Sex Shop Time Trial. I would have come up with a much better name. (Once 'The Road Trip' episode airs, people send me messages on Twitter asking if the Sex Shop Time Trial route can be added to Strava.)

After watching Annemiek van Vleuten and Warren Barguil conquer the Izoard we descend to our base in Saint-Chaffrey and head to a restaurant called Le Triptyque to record the podcast. It has the ambience of a cocktail bar and the food is a French take on tapas. I can't decide between the grilled octopus and the black pudding, so I order both and keep a close eye on François when the black pudding arrives.

Friday, 21 July

Stage 19: Embrun–Salon-de-Provence, 222.5km
Stage winner: Edvald Boasson Hagen
Yellow jersey: Chris Froome

We make our final service station stop of the Tour. The peculiar routine of stopping to fill the car with fuel and ourselves with food is almost at an end. Every day we see colleagues, team press officers and bus drivers at the services. Some I chat to, others I'm on only nodding terms with, but the Tour de France accreditation badge, worn around our necks almost non-stop for three weeks, bonds us together somehow. A Dutch colleague and I roll our eyes at the shoddy selection of sandwiches and snacks on display. There's the same demoralising browse through the familiar brand of packaged sandwiches, all of which taste of fridge and disappointment. I even raise my eyebrows slightly to say hello to Irritating Belgian Radio Man, knowing I probably won't see him again until the Classics.

This is a poor choice of stop, although it's always a game of roulette because you never know what will be on offer until you're in the slip road and can see the signs. There's only one area serving food, the queue is long and slow-moving. Richard, sensing I am on the verge of cracking, switches on the recorder and we try to capture the sounds of this bizarre ritual.

I notice that François's mask of urbane sophistication has slipped. He's hurriedly, and rather guiltily, eating a packet of processed mini salami pieces. Not the sort of thing I'd expect him to enjoy. He shrugs. 'The Tour drives you to do some strange things.'

Edvald Boasson Hagen wins the stage after he and Nikias Arndt shook off the other riders in the break by taking the shortest line through a roundabout at a critical point in the finale. I'm pleased for him because I think back to the charming and philosophical way he accepted defeat at Nuits-Saint-Georges, when Marcel Kittel beat him by the width of a sheet of paper (or thereabouts). His mum and dad had arrived just in time to see the finish and when they greeted their son I saw how their pride far outweighed their disappointment and thought that was an example for everyone.

After the stage, François heads home to Marseille and Richard, Simon and I go to our hotel. It's on the outskirts of Aix-en-Provence, a fabulous town, but we are just too far outside to walk in and it's too late to organise a taxi, so we settle for a mediocre meal in the soulless hotel restaurant.

Saturday, 22 July

Stage 20: Marseille–Marseille, 22.5km
Stage winner: Maciej Bodnar
Yellow jersey: Chris Froome

The idea of having the start and finish of the time trial in the Stade Velodrome, home to Olympique Marseille, seemed a good one on paper

Froome time trialling in Marseille

but now I am standing inside the stadium I'm not so sure. There had been reports that 50,000 tickets had been shifted but as La Course gets underway the 67,000-seat arena is a quarter full, at best. Although it does fill up a bit as the afternoon goes on the atmosphere is like a preliminary round game in the Europa League.

It's a shame to be so critical but there seems to be a reluctance to put the professional bike riders centre stage and a desire instead to divert the crowd's attention to almost anything else. There's a dreadful DJ playing generic music that would clear the dance floor at any provincial nightclub and a pair of BMX stunt riders doing underwhelming tricks on a half-pipe. The big screen doesn't even show the women's race until the riders reach the hill.

It does improve a bit later on, and the reception for Barguil and Bardet is spine-tingling. I wonder what it would have been like if the place had been full. The crowd boo Froome, although these feel like pantomime boos rather than venomous ones. Anyway, he's no Chris Waddle, is he?

Overall, we have to put this one down as a failed experiment. As Daniel will tell us, cycling is just not a stadium sport.

I bump into Greg and Kathy LeMond outside the stadium – it's the first time I've seen them the whole Tour – and their enthusiasm for the race, for France and life in general gives me a boost after the slightly sapping experience inside.

By the time we reach our hotel, round the corner from the old port in Marseille, it's past nine. François has booked a restaurant to round off our Tour in style but it's forty minutes away and our taxi has not turned up. I am tired and I start to wonder why we can't just walk to the port and find a restaurant there.

We're heading to a place called Le Chateau at Sormiou, south of the city on a remote stretch of coast. Even the taxi driver, when he finally arrives, seems reluctant to take us, despite the fact his meter is ticking over at a cadence even Chris Froome would struggle to match.

The hidden gem at Sormiou

When we arrive, I realise why François had been so keen to bring us here. It's not quite dark yet so we can see the beautiful little *calanque*, or inlet, down below us. It's rocky and dramatic and the road, if we can call it that, leading down to the water zig-zags dramatically. We dine outside on exquisite fish as the sun finally bids adieu and the moon takes its place. François explains that his mother's ashes are scattered out there somewhere and that he'd like to go the same way. I can see why it would be the perfect place for an eternal rest after a long tour.

We present François with a modest thank you gift for his company. It's a bottle of pastis, although I've failed to get him his preferred brand. That's just how we roll on *The Cycling Podcast*, François. We strive for 60 per cent accuracy in all things.

I feel quite sad, all of a sudden, that this is the end of our Tour but it's been such good fun and I hope that François will be able to join us again.

Sunday, 23 July

Stage 21: Montgeron–Paris, 103km
Stage winner: Dylan Groenewegen
Yellow jersey: Chris Froome

On the way to the airport we stop to fill up, and empty out, the hire car. Richard does the fuel and I fling open the doors and boot and start tidying. There are newspapers and Tour de France results sheets, water bottles and sandwich packets, at least one bag that once contained little salami pieces (which suggests François may have been developing a secret habit) and the detritus of three weeks on the road.

It feels surreal to be flying home from Marseille knowing we're skipping Paris but I can't say I am particularly sorry. I have a funny relationship with the capital when it comes to the Tour because it always feels like an anti-climax.

For three weeks the Tour has taken over wherever it has been. People hang up bunting and make welcoming signs. They paint old bikes in yellow, green and polka-dots and prop them on roundabouts. Farmers arrange their hay bales into bicycle shapes. And then we arrive in Paris, often after a long transfer, which makes the sense of detachment even more pronounced, and it feels like it doesn't belong. The excitement and spectacle at close quarters are undeniable but stroll a block away from the race and there's almost no evidence the world's greatest sporting event is taking place.

For the riders, it must feel like the last day of school term before the holidays and they're just waiting for the bell to ring. They just want to greet their loved-ones and get on with the party and then go home. Not long after the podium presentations have concluded it feels like the bubble we've been living in for the past three weeks has burst.

I also won't miss the traditional eye-wateringly expensive Parisian lunch. The highlight from past years is spending €30 on a salade de concombre, which was accompanied by a thimble-sized glass of white wine. The salad consisted only of peeled cucumber that had been sliced so thinly I had to admire the chef's knife skills, arranged so it covered the plate and decorated with a Jackson Pollock-esque dribble of yoghurt dressing.

Instead, I am home in time to watch the stage on television and make a start on my washing.

13. LA COURSE DIARY

Orla Chennaoui

Briançon, 19 July

The Frenchwoman shuffling across the sunlit courtyard in front of me was sprightly for an eighty-six-year-old. Dragging my case, I was struggling to keep up. This was the home straight in my 1200km journey by plane, taxi and car hire to the French Alps on the eve of La Course. It was also my first opportunity to sample *The Cycling Podcast*'s famous love of the good life.

'We've done our time in Formules 1,' Richard explained to me after a previous Tour de France, when I remarked on his good humour after three usually soul-sapping weeks on the road. 'We make sure we stay in places where we'll enjoy the races, not endure them.'

Sounded promising. With Briançon's hotels full, he had arranged an Airbnb for me.

From the top of the stairs, Madame yelled: *'Je ne peux pas bouger comme avant ma fille'* – 'I can't move like I used to.' Was she mocking me?

'But I did change the bed sheets for you,' she continued. 'We had some cyclists staying. Sweaty bunch they were. Men, the lot of them. *Ouais*, I'm a bit slow these days but I can still change a bed sheet.'

As I was still bumping my case up the final steps, Madame opened the front door and it all made sense. She was so proud of having changed the bed sheets because it meant that there was, at least, a bed. But that was about it. Almost everything in this one-bedroom apartment had been sold off, it transpired, under the entrepreneurial eye of Madame's son-in-law.

As Madame closed the door, I took a look around my would-be home for the next few days and I will admit I was disappointed. In myself. In my early twenties I would have embraced the adventure. But I'm too far into my thirties to be charmed by cold showers and eating on the floor when I'll be on the go for up to eighteen hours a day.

I call my sister-in-law who had moved to the area a few months earlier and tell her how much I can't wait to see her new home, and that yes, a sofa bed would be wonderful, thank you. Then I lug that bloody suitcase back down three flights of stairs. I am here to enjoy this bike race after all, not endure it.

Briançon, 20 July

La Course stage 1: Briançon–Col d'Izoard, 67.5km
Winner: Annemiek van Vleuten

Early morning

The day broke bright but cloudy. It was warm but not hot, fresh but not windy. I was buoyed by a good night's sleep in a colour-coordinated room, and a dinner with the podcast gents much more in keeping with their reassuringly high standards.

This was to be the first time La Course would be run over two days, and the route and format of the event had been the subject of much speculation and considerable tweaking. Since its inception in 2014, it had been a one-day race, essentially a kermesse or criterium, around the streets of Paris on the final day of the Tour. The argument was that this gave women's racing a platform like no other. The problem was that the media and fans were all there for the biggest bike race in the world, not the sprint before.

When ASO announced that La Course would be revamped in 2017,

LA COURSE DIARY   157

the speculation was that they were going to deliver on the demand for a three-day race, perhaps with mountain, time trial and sprint stages. This was based on nothing other than wishful thinking, so it should have been no surprise that the announcement, when it came, was at first underwhelming. La Course was to remain a one-day race, but it was to move from Paris to the Alps and have its first mountain-top finish. As mouth-watering a prospect as the Col d'Izoard was, the sprinters' race had simply become a climbers' race. And a short one at that. At 67km, compared with 179.5km for the men, ASO were seen by some to have insulted the ambitions and abilities of the women's peloton.

Six months later, a second day's racing was added, in an unprecedented pursuit format. The top twenty finishers on the Izoard would race on the same 22.5km time trial course as the men in Marseille two days later, starting with the time gaps they had gained on the mountain. Unlike in the Alps, however, in Marseille the women would not be racing for World Tour points, but . . . well, what exactly? Honour? Media exposure? The uncertainty provoked suspicion that the women's race was to serve as little more than entertainment, rather than add a meaningful race to the calendar.

That feeling shifted noticeably after the inaugural men's Hammer Series in early May, which was similarly innovative and surprisingly exciting. Also, by the time we reached the foot of the Izoard on the morning of day one of La Course, there was a feeling that maybe shorter was better after all. Stage 13 of the Tour de France six days earlier, served up just 101km and delivered arguably the most exciting racing of the Tour.

Given the hype and controversy, it was a race not to be ignored or reported on from afar, and so it was that I came to find myself waiting outside my sister-in-law's house for the Mystery Machine to roll into view. This was the nickname Simon, the photographer, and I had given to his VW camper the night before, in honour of the cartoon Scooby Doo. I'm almost sure there was a good reason for it at the time. He was to be Shaggy, me Velma, Richard Scrappy, on account of his physique. Lionel was Daphne. She was the only other Scooby Doo character we could think of. Sorry, Lionel. François escaped this childish nonsense by dint of having official Tour duties to perform at the start line.

I will admit to being a little giddy. Bike racing makes me that way. The boys were running late and I was practically hopping by the time the Mystery Machine rolled into view. I jumped in as the door was sliding open. 'Mooooooorniiiiiiiing! High five, Shaggy!' Simon smiled and gamely obliged from the driver's seat. 'Why, hello there, Scrappy!' Richard looked at me strangely. 'Huh?'

I tried Lionel: 'And how are you then, Daphne?' Silence. By the time I'd settled into the back of the van, I was aware of a distinct disconnect between my mood and everybody else's.

It turned out there had been a minor disagreement en route over the one bone of contention certain to divide any group following on the heels and wheels of a bike race: food. Richard had been running late, so Lionel and Simon decided, very sensibly, to stage a supermarket raid. Simon was filling his basket when Richard realised they were in danger of getting stuck on the wrong side of the road closures. No time for food, he declared; they had to go. Keen listeners to the podcast will appreciate Richard's bravery, or foolhardiness, in standing between Lionel and his saucisson breakfast baguette.

So there was a bit of an atmosphere as we drove towards Briançon and the Col d'Izoard. We made it through the road closures without incident – and still without food. Finally, halfway up the Izoard, our oasis came in the form of a lone pension with a suspiciously empty terrace but an invitingly open front door.

Apologising for my earlier chirpiness as we crossed the car park, I recounted a story from a previous work trip where a colleague had complained to our production manager that my good humour was 'starting to grate'. Explaining that he 'wasn't a morning person,' he went on to ask our manager to 'tell Orla not to speak to me until I'm ready.'

'Well,' I was telling Richard and Simon as we crossed the threshold of the pension, 'I told the production manager to tell him to go and FUUU——' the words were still leaving my mouth when I caught sight of the woman standing inside the doorway, staring, open-mouthed, at Richard and me. Then she spoke: 'You're the guys from *The Cycling Podcast*! I listen all the time. I just knew I recognised your voice, Orla! You must be Richard?'

Oops.

Col d'Izoard, mid-morning

The summit of the Col d'Izoard is as magnificent a place as you can visit in the Alps. Today, with the sun puncturing the clouds, the slopes spattered with clashing Lycra and polished carbon, and pop music shocking the still air, was a day to remember why you love this sport. There weren't many journalists up there when we got there, but it didn't really matter. The main thing was that a top women's race would be televised, in all the countries showing the Tour de France, from start to finish.

And 67km away, at the foot of the mountain in Briançon, it was about to get underway. One hundred and nineteen riders leaned over their handlebars, chatting to left and right to still the chatter of the minds, adjusting sunglasses as the only protection of the privacy of inner thoughts and fears for the riding ahead.

The race was aggressive from the off. Charlotte Bavard, the French champion, made her move shortly after the fall of the flag, but the Dutch-based world number one team Boels Dolmans kept her on a tight rein. Rozanne Slik of Sunweb and Linda Villumsen of Veloconcept took their chances next, but once again the swarm of orange swallowed them up. Villumsen went again and she was still holding on out front as they began the climb. Behind her, Lizzie Deignan was playing the part of the storming general leading her teammate Megan Guarnier up the Izoard.

'Looks like Deignan is working for the team rather than going for the win,' said Lionel on the podcast.

'True,' I replied, 'but even Lizzie Deignan doing a lot of hard work doesn't necessarily mean she might not go for it herself . . . she can still drive it from the front, you never know'.

In the end we were both right, of sorts.

Deignan did attack off the front when she realised Guarnier didn't have the form for the win, but it was too late, and too much energy had been expended. Villumsen was caught with 9km to go and, 4km later, Annemiek van Vleuten rose from her saddle. I had got to know Van Vleuten the previous year at the Rio Olympics. Nobody who saw her crash on the descent into Copacabana on the final lap of the Olympic road race will forget the horror. Having overcooked the corner, she catapulted over her handlebars, and lay slumped on the ground, head twisted, motionless for several minutes. When I interviewed her the day after her release from hospital in Rio, I expected to still see the shock of what had happened in her eyes, to find a young woman grateful to be alive. Yet even with the stitches fresh above her eye, she seemed annoyed that I wanted to talk about the crash – she preferred, even then, with her injuries so raw, to look ahead. Eleven months later, when she crossed the summit of the Col d'Izoard, and raised her arms, her smile was more than that of a winner. She was a survivor. Whether she liked it or not.

The mood 43 seconds later when Deignan crossed the line was completely different. Riding through the journalists and *soigneurs*, there was no stopping for a chat. I had a moment of blind panic as it looked as though she was going to roll all the way down the other side of the mountain without saying a word into my recorder. I decided to give chase, in my wedge-heels. Not all split-second decisions in the chaos of a race finish make sense. Mercifully, she stopped just before the second corner on the descent. By the time I caught up, so too had Guarnier. The tension was palpable. When a race has gone well teammates sometimes remind me of excited teenagers on a school trip, talking over the top of one another. 'Did you see when I . . . ?' 'I didn't even know they had . . . !' 'I can't believe you . . . '. On this occasion, not a word was spoken. Water was gulped silently from *bidons*. The air was thick with thoughts unvoiced. Both riders eventually made their way back towards the top of the climb, for the second time. Once again, they came to a stop next to each other. Once again, they didn't chat. It was obvious Lizzie rankled at sacrificing her chance of a win for a teammate who wasn't capable of finishing the job.

'Megan put her hand up and said she could be the leader,' Deignan told me, her teammate standing just behind her left shoulder. 'I perhaps did a bit too much work because we wanted Megan to go for it. I messed up by being a *domestique* and then a leader, I did too much work today. But that's cycling, that's how it goes sometimes.'

Guarnier wasn't so far off the pace that her race had been a disaster. She finished fourth, 1 minute 28 seconds behind Van Vleuten, but she was 55 seconds behind Deignan, with the Englishwoman now having 43 seconds to try to make up two days later. The Italian Elisa Longo Borghini was third, 1 minute 23 seconds off the lead.

At least as important as the result was how it had played out as a race. Speaking to other riders as they stood on the finish line, straddling the border between freshly lived experience and hardened memory, when only the sharper fragments of the day pierce through the cloud of chatter, there seemed to be the feeling of a good race, well fought. As the mountaintop grew busier, and the throng of people ever more purposeful, the general feeling was that the Col d'Izoard had been a success.

But from the highs of the Izoard, the peloton was brought back to earth with a thud. Sharing the climb was to be one of the few aspects of the day the female and male riders would have in common. While the men would retreat to the luxury of their buses, complete with toilets, showers and on-board kitchen, the women's post-race debrief took place in a public car park, halfway down the mountain.

Without thinking of the need for female riders to have somewhere private to change, there was no option for these elite athletes but to strip in full view of anyone who cared to watch. Showers would have to wait. As the riders jerked and jiggled into fresh clothes in an attempt to preserve dignity, their *directeurs sportifs* were busy booking flights. Only now did they know who had made the cut for the pursuit two days later, and who would be going home. Indeed, bosses on some teams had been looking for flights in team cars on the way up the Izoard, even as their riders were being dropped on the climb. The novelty of the new race format was one thing, the cost to teams another. They were literally paying the price of this scheduling gamble. The question was, would it be worth it?

Embrun, 21 July, morning

A 222.5km race route from Embrun to Salon de Provence for the Tour de France, and a 260km transfer from Briançon to Marseille for La Course. There was little reason for me to drive to Embrun and add several hours to my journey, other than a compulsion to be near to the action.

Embrun was set up as most Tour start/finish towns are, that is to say with a mass of road closures and diversions and the colonisation of the largest car park in the vicinity. The sun was unrelenting as hundreds of fans wandered around the temporary fences encircling the team buses. While cycling is still one of the most accessible sports, ticketed enclosures have become increasingly common. Today, I was technically a spectator since my accreditation didn't cover the stage. I had two secret weapons at my disposal, however: yesterday's accreditation hanging from its distinctive yellow lanyard around my neck, and Richard's folding Brompton bike. The latter became necessary when I realised I had no vehicle pass for the day, and that a smile and some French compliments would only get me so close to the start of the race. Fortunately, the sight of a mini-skirted woman bumping along on an outsized bike was enough of a peculiarity for the gendarme manning the entrance to wave me and my duplicitous pass through without close inspection.

Inside the compound, packed with team buses and vehicles, I wondered where the few dozen vehicles of the women's peloton would have been parked, had they been here. Crowded as the space was, there was still room enough to accommodate the entirety of the women's entourage. Had the much wished for three stages of La Course gone ahead, this would have been the sprint day. Commentators would have had several hours of racing to talk about before the men's stage, and all the nervous, excited tension of Le Tour would have had a positive outlet, satisfying impatient race cravings.

Having eventually made myself useful and presented the final Pédaleur de Charme T-shirt of the Tour to the very worthy and suitably delighted Warren Barguil, I was back in the car and, after two hours of waiting for the roads to reopen, finally en route to Marseille.

Warren Barguil, Pédaleur de Charme

Embrun-Marseille, 20 July, afternoon

One of the pleasures for me of being part of a race caravan is perhaps some people's idea of hell on four wheels: the close proximity of human company and the random, meandering conversations which that intimacy encourages. In the days of smartphones and 4G, it is a luxury to switch off from technology and take the time to empty one's brain of conversation. I've learned many a surprising fact and facet of a companion's personality and history from travelling in the rolling confessional of a bike race hire-car. This time, though, there was no one to swap stories with, no one to argue with over music selection. It was just me, the local radio DJ and some Euro pop. I admit to being quite partial to a touch of Mylene Farmer and Enrique Iglesias. With no one to bear witness to the horror, I was free to throw off the shackles of social convention and sing with all the talent and power the good Lord gave me. We were stuck just outside Embrun in a typical Tour traffic jam and as I opened my eyes after a particularly challenging high note, I saw that Lionel, sitting in the car in front, was mockingly dancing along to my silent disco.

I switched stations, which led to one of my best Tour de France discoveries. Listening to the Tour unfold on French radio is to step into an almost antiquated world of story-telling, history and passion. I was captivated. Recently retired bike riders like Jérôme Pineau describe the action of the race. A chat with Warren Barguil's father fills the air space usually occupied by castles and cornfields. If you speak the language, and you've never managed to listen on French radio, I strongly urge you to do so. As timing would have it, I was just approaching the port of Marseille's old town, trying to locate my hotel when the audio-waves crescendoed for the first stage win of this year's Tour for its nearly man, Edvald Boasson Hagen. If one day we could enjoy a fraction of that excitement, a tiny slice of that air time for women's racing, we'll have come a long way indeed.

Marseille, 22 July

La Course stage 2: Marseille, 22.5km time trial
Winner: Annemiek van Vleuten

If stage 1 of La Course was humbling in the grandeur of its setting, stage 2 was a leveller, a prosaic return to earth. For the team buses, cars and media, the day was to be spent mostly in the concrete surroundings of the car park adjacent to the Stade Vélodrome. The bulky finery of the men's paddock impressed in its size and sheen, squatting brutely across the expanse of tarmac. Swarms of sponsors, fans and hangers-on buzzed around hundreds of freshly polished vehicles, manoeuvring beneath unfurled awnings for shade. At one end of the car park, on the right-hand side as you leave the stadium, sat the women's mini-paddock, a few dozen team cars and small campervans, many with deck chairs set up outside. With temperatures of over 30 degrees Celsius, and the heat chasing any lingering clouds away, it was to be a brutal day to be seeking solace from parasols and ice boxes.

By now, I am back to working my day job for Sky Sports News, primarily covering the final stages of the Tour de France, rather than La Course. As I fumble online for any live streaming or race updates while hunkered in the shade of a mechanics' truck between live broadcasts, I ask Richard for a personal race commentary from inside the stadium. It turns out he and Lionel are just as much in the dark inside the venue as I am outside it. After the race took to the streets of Marseille, the much-hyped part two of La Course – which is definitely not just a sideshow and is absolutely an integral part of today's racing action – barely lights the filaments of the Stade's display screens. Instead, the huge TVs show the stadium DJ alongside a BMX stunt rider performing in the venue.

As goodness-knew-what was happening on the road, I tried to get myself in a position to cover the post-race reaction. Unfortunately, after almost three weeks on the road, frazzled race officials neither knew the rider protocol after the race, nor seemed to really care. After asking several T-shirted members of staff of varying job descriptions, it became clear that tracking down anyone to interview on leaving the velodrome was going to be a combination of luck, nimble feet and 20/20 vision.

Going on timing alone, I knew the race must be coming to an end, and began running up, down and around a maze of outer walkways which hug the stadium. Through one bag-check, I sprinted up a staircase to try to catch anything that would help inform my post-race interviews. I caught the briefest of glimpses of a TV screen which, unlike the large screens inside the venue, was showing live coverage of the race. Just in time I see Annemiek Van Vleuten cross the line first, then I sprint back downstairs. Knowing the other riders will be arriving into and then swiftly exiting the stadium, I struggle to find an obvious route for them to follow, and for me to intercept. Back through the bag-check, I wait at the closest exit and look down the long tunnel to the field of play. There's no one in sight and not much of a feeling of anything happening, so I run to the next one. This doesn't feel quite right either. I decide to cut my losses and run back to the team car park, all the time aware that my two-wheeled targets could be lost to me already. Sod's law, this is where I should have stayed all along.

It turns out I'm not the only one running around like a 'poule sans tête'. Having set up our camera equipment next to the team cars, I spot Lizzie Deignan riding towards our camera spot, bouquet of podium flowers in hand, having finished second once again. I congratulate her and ask for an interview, but she is initially more concerned with apologising. 'I was really rude to Lia earlier, can you please apologise for me?' She was referring to my friend and producer Lia Hervey, but about what, I had no idea. It turns out that Lia had approached Lizzie before the race, asking for a quick interview about the stage ahead. Lizzie, however, had been trying to find a toilet for 45 minutes and was desperate by the time a TV camera was in front of her face.

As for the race itself, Van Vleuten's advantage was too much to create

For captions, see page 249

any suspense. If anything, her time trialling is stronger than her climbing. The only wisp of a question was whether Deignan would try to catch her alone or wait for the next brace of riders starting behind her. This was her strategy and with Longo Borghini and Guarnier she hunted down Van Vleuten, but in vain. It was a bit of an anti-climax, even for the winner. 'For me, the real win was on the Izoard,' Van Vleuten told Richard for the podcast, 'that was the real race.'

La Course stage 2 had been a laudable experiment at best, a half-hearted after-thought at worst. There was that itchy, scraggy feeling of a job half done. We could almost see what the racing could have been, and were all the more frustrated by what it wasn't. 'It's been a fun event to be part of,' concluded Deignan, 'but I think fun is the right word for it at the moment.'

P.S. Two weeks after I had returned from La Course and the Tour, an email popped up in my inbox. It was a feedback comment from the owners of the Airbnb in Briançon, forwarded by Richard: 'The state of the apartment was incredibly clean, such that you couldn't even be sure if the bed had been slept in.'

14. VUELTA A ESPAÑA DIARY: WEEK 1

Richard Moore

Friday, 18 August, Nîmes

So here we go again, barely 100km from where my last Grand Tour ended in Marseille after the penultimate stage of the Tour de France. Nîmes is a small city, the perfect size for a Vuelta start, and the teams' presentation is just right. Not flash or glitzy, but not exactly understated, it's held in Les Jardins de la Fontaine, ten minutes' walk from the centre. In the middle of the gardens there's a stage and a few hundred people are seated and clap politely as the teams are introduced.

Away to the left of the stage, in a large, dusty expanse of ground beneath a protective canopy of trees, circles of ten seats are arranged for the teams. Some do sit together, like tight units – Orica are one, Aqua Blue another. But most riders get up and mingle. Sitting on a wall are an assortment of Italians from Sky, Bahrain-Merida and Quick-Step Floors. The mood is relaxed.

I speak to Joe Dombrowski and Michael Woods of Cannondale-Drapac, both sporting severe Grand Tour haircuts. 'We went to the same place today,' says Joe. Woods, who always seems to be restless, and bursting with curiosity, suddenly asks, 'Hey, have you watched *Icarus?*'

He's talking about the documentary, just out, that reveals the scale of Russia's state-organised doping programme. His thoughts on it are interesting. The film actually began as an attempt by the film-maker, a keen amateur cyclist, to follow a hardcore doping programme to compete in a multi-day sportive in the Alps. The assumption often, when it comes to cycling, seems to be that doping explains everything: that there is no performance ceiling for someone prepared to dope. Which ignores lots of other things that go into a performance, such as talent. Like a lot of people, Woods found that aspect, and the assumptions behind it, irritating but, overall, he found the film fascinating and shocking on a whole new level. 'Basically,' he says, 'if you were Russian, you doped.'

'But some people think that about professional cyclists – they would say that of all the riders doing the Vuelta,' I say.

Woods and Dombrowski look dismayed at that. One big story on the eve of the race is a positive test for the 2008 Olympic road race champion, Samuel Sanchez. He's the biggest name snared in quite some time. Woods is disgusted. 'You know, they talk about Spain's golden generation: Valverde, Contador, Sanchez. Valverde busted in Operation

Puerto, Contador had a positive test, and now Sanchez. Golden generation? You know, I wish these guys would just disappear.'

Later, Contador, soon to retire, is introduced on stage. A short film is played, a tribute to his career. We're in France, so Warren Barguil gets the biggest cheer, but for Contador, ahead of his farewell tour, there is warm, heartfelt appreciation. To speak ill of Contador over the next three weeks will be tantamount to blasphemy. As Woods says, it's remarkable, really.

Saturday, 19 August

Stage 1: Nîmes, team time trial, 13.7km
Stage winner: BMC
Red jersey: Rohan Dennis

Lionel and I have lunch in a restaurant by the amphitheatre. We're near the exit, from which the teams will emerge after whizzing through the centre of the arena.

It's a stunning setting, though, as I tell Lionel, it's a shame parts of the amphitheatre are covered in scaffolding. 'It's two thousand years old!' he says. It's a fair point, so I resist correcting him (it's 1,947 years old).

The race is in a few hours and the teams warm up. This is their first chance to ride the course on closed roads (Marco Pinotti, BMC's time trial coach, has ridden it at 5am the previous four mornings.) Most teams do two laps. The circuit is tight and twisty before the entry to the arena and technical on the way out, too. And since nobody wants to mess up the showpiece part of the stage – or, indeed, any part – they ride in formation, and at speed, on entry and exit.

Lunch (tuna steak) is rudely interrupted by (literally) a CRASH and a BANG followed by a lot of shouting and swearing. As Quick-Step swung out of the arena they met a car. It was crawling towards them but shouldn't have been there at all. The reaction down the line causes David

The amphitheatre at Nîmes

de la Cruz to touch a wheel and go down; we hear brakes squealing and angry recriminations. This chaotic scene is mirrored outside the restaurant as diners leap to their feet and rush to the barriers – with the sole exception of Lionel, who carries on tucking into his tuna. What a pro. De la Cruz is OK; he remounts and Quick-Step carry on.

But a few minutes later there's another scare. We don't see this one – it happens inside the tunnel coming out of the arena – but we hear the chaos and observe just one Cannondale-Drapac rider emerging. The others appear in dribs and drabs, with Joe Dombrowski last. He

The aftermath of a crash during team time trial practice

studies his bike and stretches his leg. He's OK too and they carry on. We hadn't expected such a dramatic lunch.

The team time trial really is spectacular: a lesson in how to open a Grand Tour, with the dash through the centre of the amphitheatre, played out before a full house (entry was free), absolutely wonderful. The Vuelta hasn't always got it right (a team time trial along a beach cycle path, anyone?) but this is a triumph.

Later, more drama as we eat dinner on the terrace of a restaurant close to the centre. News reaches us that Nîmes is 'in lockdown', with three armed terrorists on the loose. Shooting is reported at the station – 480 metres away, according to Google Maps. We lift our meal-time mobile phone ban. This proves a mistake. While we anxiously refresh our Twitter feeds, the streets remain curiously filled with diners, all apparently oblivious. Meanwhile, some reports (notably in a couple of British newspapers) become ever more hysterical: gunmen are roaming

Waiting for the gladiators to appear

the streets, they tell us; just days after the Barcelona attacks, Nîmes is believed to be under siege by terrorists.

Later, we learn the facts: that there had been a troubled man on board a train with what was believed to be either a toy gun or starter pistol. It's sobering to find ourselves at the centre of a fake news story. Sad!

Sunday, 20 August

Stage 2: Nîmes–Gruissan, Grand Narbonne, 203.4km
Stage winner: Yves Lampaert
Red jersey: Yves Lampaert

This has the feel of a stage that exists entirely to get the riders from one point to another, a little closer to Spain. And yet the wind makes it a little more than that. It's blowing a hoolie, as we say in Scotland. That makes it fraught, and absolutely set up for a Quick-Step smash-n-grab. A bit like stage 3 of the Giro on Sardinia, when the wind blew and Bob Jungels tore the race to shreds to set up Fernando Gaviria, here there is a different cast but the same outcome: Matteo Trentin did the Jungels job and then Yves Lampaert clipped off the front to win alone, with Trentin second.

The stage was so fast there was not a single breakaway; there were eighty-five roundabouts to negotiate; and it was a baptism of fire for Aqua Blue Sport, whose riders appear back at the bus looking quite traumatised. Yet one of them, Adam Blythe, who'd tipped himself for the win the previous day, does well to finish third. An excellent result for the Irish team, and Lionel tries to bask in a little of their glory, with the revelation that he used to 'race with' one of their riders, Conor Dunne. The quotation marks are mine.

Today and until we are in Spain we are travelling with Fran Reyes, a Spanish journalist who will give our Vuelta coverage some much-needed youthful vigour. Fran is twenty-five but this alone cannot explain his energy levels (we should have done what some teams insist on, and checked his biological passport). He does everything at 100mph, including – or so it feels like – driving. When he's not running after people and engaging them in earnest conversation, he's learning Chinese, or singing. I thought Fran's company would make me feel younger. Now I'm not so sure.

Monday, 21 August, Andorra

Stage 3: Prades–Andorra, 158.5km
Stage winner: Vincenzo Nibali
Red jersey: Chris Froome

'We're in Andorra,' says Lionel, opening tonight's podcast, 'the worst place in Europe.'

Andorra

Yet it's the in-vogue place for pro cyclists: the new Girona. Indeed, many ex-Girona residents now live here, enjoying the thin air, the tax-free status, and associated benefits such as (I imagine) cheap 200-packs of cigarettes and litre bottles of spirits. Lionel might be exaggerating, but only slightly. It has even less going for it than Monaco, which at least has the sea and a beach. There are beautiful mountains surrounding Andorra, but you can't really see them for the tall, tasteless buildings.

I think we are scarred by our visit during the previous year's Tour, when we spent a rest day here. We couldn't get our washing done in the one, very small launderette. The roads were clogged up with (admittedly mainly Tour) traffic. Everything was expensive (apart from fags and spirits). Our phones didn't work, except to allow me to receive two calls from home, which, when I later studied my bill, came to about £48.

At least on this occasion the stage is exciting. The Shark of Messina wins, despite Sky's game plan being specifically designed to drop Nibali, who tends to become more dangerous in the third week; today he is dropped on the climb but gets back on and takes a clever win. But the big story is that, while Gianni Moscon was setting the pace on the climb, Contador slid off the back and lost more than two minutes. At the finish, El Pistolero looks as happy to be arriving in Andorra as Lionel.

Tuesday, 22 August

Stage 4: Escaldes-Engordany–Tarragona, 158.5km
Stage winner: Matteo Trentin
Red jersey: Chris Froome

Lionel and I are standing outside the Orica-Scott bus because Lionel wants to interview Mat Hayman.
'Let's go,' I say.
'We can't,' says Lionel.
'Why not?'
'We're waiting for Hayman.'
'Ah!'
The wait goes on. Riders come and go. It's hot. There's no shade. Eventually I say, 'I can't go on like this.'
'That's what you think,' says Lionel.
We spot Filippo Pozzato, walking out of one of Andorra's fancy malls in the company of a *domestique*, who looks downtrodden and is carrying Pozzato's shopping bags, full of tax-free designer watches. Pozzato is imperious, full of confidence and bluster; he and his *domestique* linger by the Orica bus, distracting us. 'I don't seem to be able . . . to depart,' says Pozzato. 'Such is life,' says Lionel. But eventually Pozzato and his *domestique* do move on.
'That passed the time,' says Lionel.
'It would have passed in any case,' I reply.

'Yes, but not so rapidly.'

OK, OK, I give up. The above is all stolen from *Waiting for Godot*, Samuel Beckett's play. Pozzato and his *domestique* weren't really there; they are stand-ins for Pozzo and Lucky, Pozzo's slave, who distract Vladimir and Estragon (Lionel and me). Lionel and I didn't spend all morning waiting outside the Orica bus for Mat Hayman. But Lionel did, having announced on his way to the start that he was going to speak to Hayman for an episode of *Kilometre 0* about the *voiture balai*, or broom wagon – the vehicle that follows the race, sweeping up dropped riders. 'Hayman's been around a bit,' said Lionel. 'He's sure to have a story or two about the broom wagon.'

The only problem is that Lionel had as much chance of interviewing Hayman as he did of interviewing Godot. Hayman is not riding the Vuelta.

'No sign of Hayman,' says Lionel when he appears back at the car a few hours later. 'I'll try him again tomorrow.'

'Are you sure he's riding?' I say. A long silence follows, broken eventually by Lionel: 'It's not my fault,' he says. 'I spilled honey on my start sheet at breakfast.'

Waiting for Godot moments are not uncommon in this job. We do spend a lot of time standing outside team buses waiting for riders who may or may not appear. But I am not aware of many occasions when I've been waiting for a rider not actually at the race.

One theory is that it was a bike race that inspired Beckett to write *Waiting for Godot*. The story goes that Beckett, who lived in Paris and wrote the play in French in the late 1940s, encountered roadside spectators at the Tour de France, who told him, 'We are waiting for Godot' – a rider named Godot, who was off the back. The counter speculation is that it was in fact Roger Godeau, a track rider in the 1940s, and that the exchange occurred outside the Roubaix velodrome rather than at the Tour de France.

Taking all this to its natural conclusion – and relating it back to Lionel's *Waiting for Hayman*, and to his quest, which was to speak to him about the broom wagon – imagine if the roadside spectators that Beckett encountered were destined to wait forever for Godot, the cyclist, because he had climbed into the broom wagon? Readers and academics have been studying Beckett's most famous play for decades trying to decipher its real meaning, but I don't think they have ever considered this: that Godot would never appear because he was in the *voiture balai*.

Wednesday, 23 August

Stage 5: Benicàssim–Alcossebre, 175.7km
Stage winner: Alexey Lutsenko
Red jersey: Chris Froome

We try to go for a decent meal in Castellón, where we're staying a second night. TripAdvisor is both the saviour and scourge of the modern tourist, and we are nothing if not modern tourists. Face inches from my phone, feeling like the Pied Piper with my companions at my heels, I follow the blue dot to one of the city's top-rated restaurants, only to end up at a closed door. So we do what we have done so many times before – what people must have done before TripAdvisor, if you can imagine such a time – and retrace our steps to a place we'd passed earlier, which Lionel said looked nice and was packed with people ('But it's only ranked 478th on TripAdvisor! Somebody found a dead cockroach in their gin and tonic!'). And we eat a very nice meal, starting with absolutely enormous tomatoes.

'Doped tomatoes,' says Daniel. He's such a cynic. To paraphrase the Controversial Lance Armstrong*, I'm sorry he doesn't believe in enormous tomatoes.

---

* This is how the disgraced Lance Armstrong is known by *The Cycling Podcast* after he complained to Daniel that he was fed up seeing his name prefixed with 'disgraced.' When Daniel asked what he would prefer, Armstrong replied: 'I dunno. Controversial?'

Thursday, 24 August

Stage 6: Villareal–Sagunto, 204.4km
Stage winner: Tomasz Marczyński
Red jersey: Chris Froome

It's a typical Vuelta stage, with nothing particularly catching the eye on the profile, only to turn into an absolute horror show for many of the riders. One, Conor Dunne, will later describe this stage as his personal hell. Alberto Contador, confirming what we thought we saw the previous day, when Fran got very upset that we didn't discuss his resurgence in the podcast, looks like a different rider to the one who limped into Andorra. Froome is the only one who can follow Contador on the steep little climbs. It's vintage Contador: out of the saddle, luring Daniel into the great Contador cliché, which brings an official warning from the 'Dancing on the Pedals' police.

The Polish one-two catches my eye, with Tomasz Marczyński first and Pawel Poljański second. 'That can't have happened before in a Grand Tour,' I assert on the podcast.

'No,' says Lionel. 'Not since Marseille about three weeks ago.' (Of course: Bodnar and Kwiatkowski in the time trial at the Tour de France.)

Tonight we bid adios to Lionel, who has a spring in his step all day. 'Last day of the Vuelta,' he keeps saying, hoping to crack me. I am staying another ten days, then he's returning for the final week of what he has dubbed 'the holiday Grand Tour'. Don't forget your bucket and spade, Lionel.

Friday, 25 August

Stage 7: Llíria–Cuenca, 207km
Stage winner: Matej Mohorič
Red jersey: Chris Froome

One of the things I most enjoy about covering a Grand Tour from beginning to end is following some of the lesser known riders. Someone catches your eye – perhaps you spot them at the finish looking sorry for themselves, or battling on with crash wounds, or maybe, more unusually, it is their cheeriness that stands out. The rider who has caught my eye here is Conor Dunne. This isn't really a surprise: at six foot eight inches, he towers over everyone. He is believed to be the tallest rider ever to ride a Grand Tour and has been christened 'El Alto' (the giant) by the Spanish press.

He is a gentle giant. I've spoken to him most days, simply because he is so honest, offering the kind of insight that most riders are unwilling, or, frankly, unable, to offer. He is also ridiculously polite, apologising for keeping you waiting and thanking you at the end. I'm cheating with this diary entry because I'm including something that I heard about weeks later. But it relates to this stage. And when I heard it, it made absolute sense.

At the finish in Cuenca there was a sombre mood around the Aqua Blue Sport bus because Larry Warbasse, their captain and Dunne's roommate, had crashed badly and was out of the race. Like everybody, Dunne was sorry about that, but it didn't fully explain the state he was in.

Much later, I learned that Dunne had broken down in tears on the bus before the stage and that some wondered if he'd even start, let alone finish. It wasn't witnessed by everybody. Warbasse didn't know, and over the radio, early in the stage, he asked Dunne why he wasn't at the front. 'Go easy on Conor,' another teammate told Warbasse, telling him what had happened on the bus. Warbasse felt terrible and immediately got back on the radio, telling Dunne not to worry, to stay where he was and look after himself.

At the finish, although I didn't know about this, it was obvious, speaking to him, that Dunne had come through a personal nightmare. He was hesitant when I asked how his day had been. 'Em, yeah, OK. It was a super hard day for me yesterday. I was on a bad day. I was suffering a lot at the back, just holding on, doing everything I could to survive. I got through in the *gruppetto* and I was proud of that. But it took a lot of mental strength.

'I had a bit of a bad moment this morning before the stage. Yesterday I had to dig so deep I really didn't know if I could do it again in my head. Luckily I had some teammates who gave me some wise words. The body is OK. Keeping the mind strong is the toughest bit.'

Dunne will be far from alone in finding the daily mental struggle the hardest part of riding a Grand Tour, but he is unusual in admitting it.

Saturday, 26 August

Stage 8: Hellín–Xorret de Catí, 199.5km
Stage winner: Julian Alaphilippe
Red jersey: Chris Froome

Stayed in a great hotel last night, the Hotel Bella Hellín, a few kilometres outside Hellín. It was a two-hour drive from Cuenca so I got there after eleven but Daniel and Scott, his cameraman, had warned the *patrón* that I would be late. Not that this usually matters in Spain, but I was especially grateful on this occasion. The place was not easy to find, at the end of a bumpy track, and the building was unprepossessing. But the food!

Gregorio and Suzanna, who run the place, serve up some eagerly-awaited

Michelin-star-standard grub. We had the tasting menu (is this not just known as 'tapas' in Spain, I did wonder) and every morsel was delicious. It was a real treat, all the more enjoyable because it was so unexpected.

Equally unexpected were the goats. I only realised that we were sleeping above goats in the morning when I went for a late breakfast. In fact, Hotel Bella Hellín is a working farm. My room, too, was exceptional: newly decorated and enormous. I was so enjoying my stay at Hotel Bella Hellín that I decided to skip the start to linger a little longer. Bliss.

It was in this relaxed state of mind that I sat at breakfast, sipping coffee, stuffing my face with delicious cheese (goat's cheese – of course!) and feeling a little smug as I watched Daniel and Scott pack up and hurry off. Aaaaaaaah. I get out my phone, scroll through Twitter. Oh, bugger. A flurry – a volley, coming at me like bullets from a machine gun – of #Vuelta17 tweets. Warren Barguil has been sent home. The darling of the Tour de France has been kicked out by Sunweb for riding his own race and refusing to 'conform to the team's goal'. For a brief moment I shrug it off. I seek to rationalise my decision to skip the start, which is about seven minutes' drive away. It's no good. I cannot convince myself that missing the start is acceptable. My conscience won't allow it. I put down my cheese, get up, hurry to my room, pack my bag, pay, leave in a cloud of dust and arrive at the start just behind Daniel and Scott.

Sunday, 27 August

Stage 9: Orihuela–El Poble Nou de Benitatxell, 174km
Stage winner: Chris Froome
Red jersey: Chris Froome

The party stage, along the Costa Blanca, through Alicante, on to the monstrosity that is Benidorm, along to Calpe, where so many teams base themselves in the winter, before finishing on top of a vicious little climb to Cumbre del Sol. At the start in Orihuela – actually nowhere near Orihuela, but on the closest beach to Orihuela, a quirk that causes Fran to miss the start – I wander through the Vuelta start village and see Australian rider Adam Hansen sitting on his own. He is waiting to be introduced to a ninety-two-year old man who does live in Orihuela: Bernardo Ruiz.

Ruiz won the 1948 Vuelta and was also the holder, until 2015, of the record for riding the most consecutive Grand Tours – in his case, twelve. It was Hansen who broke the record, and he's still extending it. This Vuelta is his nineteenth Grand Tour in a row. When Ruiz approaches, Hansen stands up and they shake hands. 'Who is this?' asks Ruiz. They pose for photographs. Even if Ruiz isn't entirely sure who Hansen is, or why he's been introduced to him, I find the encounter – also the fact that Hansen waited so long to meet Ruiz, and pretended not to hear Ruiz ask who he was – quite moving.

Grand Tour record-holder Adam Hansen with Bernardo Ruiz

I drive the course: roads lined with people in swimwear who have just left the beach to watch the race pass. It's strange to see Calpe in-season. I've been here lots of times in January or February to interview riders, when the town is deserted and the only sound is that of professional riders clip-clopping across polished marble lobbies in otherwise empty hotels. I think I prefer the quiet – and the cool, cloudless sunny days – of January to the heat and crowds of August.

15. VUELTA A ESPAÑA DIARY: WEEK 2

Fran Reyes

Monday, 28 August

Rest day, Murcia

On a rest day I experience 'tissular strike'. After ten straight days of non-stop working, constantly connected to the race, invaded by social media, dependent on the telephone, my mind is really at its limit. *Men sana in corpore sano*. When we reach this day with the prefix 'rest', the synapses stop firing for about twenty-four hours, until the start of the following stage.

I wake up in Alicante.

The first duty of the day was to attend Team Sky's hotel. We, the journalists, were told to convene at their humongous 'race hub' for a media day: a round of interviews that resemble speed-dating. The riders sit at their tables and the journalists come and go with a fixed amount of time to seduc—I mean, interview.

I was due to speak to Gianni Moscon. This season I have been struck both by his sporting qualities and his misbehaviour. The racist language he used towards Kévin Reza at the Tour de Romandie earned him condemnation and a punishment from his team. With Moscon riding so well in this Vuelta, working hard at the front on the climbs in support of his team leader Chris Froome during the first week of the race, it was logical that we should discuss the issue on the podcast.

Anyway: Moscon came across to me as a perfectly normal and friendly twenty-three-year-old fella. He wasn't enthusiastic, but that's normal at 11am and after nine straight days of racing. My speed-interview finished before I could ask him about the incident with Reza, but I brought it up with him off the record. He wasn't amused, but answered firmly and stuck with what has already been published.

Later on that morning I spoke to Julian Alaphilippe, then a very friendly and funny interview with Adam Yates. And, miracle, by 3pm I was done with my Vuelta work. So was Víctor, my fellow journalist and travelling companion. We had a whole afternoon and evening before us in Villamolina de Segura, the industrial town on the outskirts of Murcia where we had booked our next hotel. Maybe we could go to the beach, as Richard did, or do a 20km run like Daniel did, or walk in the small hours after dinner to just look up and contemplate the stars . . .

Nah. I lay down on the bed until the sun was gone, then resumed working. I kept at it until 6am. During those hours of late-night writing I heard heavy rain showers outside . . .

Tuesday, 29 August

Stage 10: Caravaca de la Cruz–ElPozo Alimentación-Alhama de Murcia, 164.8km
Stage winner: Matteo Trentin
Red jersey: Chris Froome

Laughing at Murcia is a running joke in Spain – it's said of Murcians that they speak bad Spanish, and that they've built on every square metre of land – but on the occasion of this visit, the joke was on the Vuelta as Murcia had its first rainy day in three months.

With my umbrella and in my waterproof jacket I went to the Movistar bus to try and get confirmation of their new women's team. This is very significant in a Spanish context. A really promising generation of female riders has emerged in a rather precarious scene where teams are at best semi-professional, most races are amateur-ish, support is scarce and coaching is poor. Some of these riders, like Sheyla Gutiérrez or Ane Santesteban, have been lucky and strong enough to land professional contracts abroad. Others never get the opportunity to develop their talent as they have to combine cycling with studies or a regular job. Eventually they grow tired of the effort and quit. Movistar's women's team will save the careers of half a dozen of these cyclists by giving them a salary, a nice racing schedule, proper assistance and counsel.

After Movistar, I went looking for Dimension Data's Igor Antón. Antón is an endearing character, kind and shy, smart and cautious, so skinny yet so strong: a good climber and stage racer who has won four Vuelta stages. I found him at the start line and he gladly agreed to an interview as long as he could shelter beneath my umbrella. When we were done recording there were still a few minutes before the start of the stage, and I felt that standing with him, under my umbrella, was the right thing to do. We chit-chatted about his collection of cycling-related magazines and newspapers, which dates back to when he was ten years old.

The peloton was lucky the rain was so heavy because it washed roads that, after many weeks without a drop of water, were dusty and tarnished with oil and dirt that would have rendered the surface slippery had the rain been lighter. That would have been especially treacherous on the descent of the Collado Bermejo, a truly daredevil road. Rubén Plaza suffered a career-threatening crash there during the Vuelta a Murcia in 2011. He misjudged a corner and fell down a cliff. One of his legs was completely shattered and he didn't have a race radio to alert his team. He had to crawl back to the road, where he was spotted by the race convoy.

As far as podcasting is concerned it was quite an unusual day. Rich suffered one of his first bouts of hip pain and didn't go to the finish, so Daniel and I headed straight to his hotel at the tiny village of El Berro to record. The landscape there was amazing, as El Berro is right in the heart of Sierra Espuña, an untamed and desolate piece of land.

I didn't enjoy the podcasting as much as the driving. I love the feeling of being behind the wheel, especially if the roads are challenging and the music is good. Sometimes I get carried away. Lionel experienced this exuberance on the drive from Andorra to Tarragona, on day three, as I was spurred on by the tunes of El Último de la Fila's 'Ya no danzo al son de los tambores'. Three times Víctor told me: 'Illo, El Guiri se nos muere' ('Buddy, the Brit is dying'). Lionel did look a little car-sick.* But there was no Víctor and no Lionel that day on the road from El Berro to Totana, and believe me, I really enjoyed myself (and El Último de la Fila) on that 30km of sharp turns under the rain.

And why was I driving to Totana? Because I was crashing at my good friend Andrés Cánovas' house. He is a cycling journalist too, nowadays acting as press officer and content creator for a couple of teams and riders. We have been good friends for years and lived the great adventure of our lives when, in 2013, we were charged to set up a UCI Continental Team in Chile. We found technical sponsors, arranged the logistics and recruited riders (including former Euskaltel riders Juan José Oroz and Pablo Urtasun) for an exciting project that turned out to be a scam. We spent ten days in Chile, some in its capital city Santiago de Chile and some in a southern, undeveloped island by the name of Chiloé, chasing the philanthropist that had lured us into an ill-fated project along with the other five Spaniards. That desperate situation created deep bonds between us. It was an unpleasant experience but one we all are glad to have endured. We didn't earn a single dime, but the reward of his friendship was priceless.

That night we had dinner at the most fancy kebab place ever – first and last time I am eating a shawarma with knife and fork.

---

* Note from Lionel: 'I wasn't car sick. I was terrified.'

Wednesday, 30 August

Stage 11: Lorca–Observatorio Astronómico de Calar Alto, 187.5km
Stage winner: Miguel Ángel López
Red jersey: Chris Froome

After troubling us on Tuesday, neither the rain nor Rich's hip offered up a truce on Wednesday. Early in the morning I got a call from Rich asking me to be his chauffeur that day, as he wasn't confident of being able to do the five hours of driving we had ahead of us. I duly put on my black hat and enjoyed steering an automatic car for the first time since 2011, when I didn't have my driving licence yet and a Geox-TMC masseur insisted I should practise with the team's luxurious Audi Q7 (I was the team's press officer). Daniel didn't savour the drive to Calar Alto that much, as he punctured along the way.

The weather was grim the whole day, a further factor to eliminate the weaker contenders. At this stage of the season, bodies and minds are squeezed like lemons. Short efforts are bearable, but longer ones take a big toll. And we could see that in Calar Alto. Out went Chaves and Aru; enter Nibali and Superman, Miguel Ángel López. The fact that Froome stood still after having ridden (and won) the Tour de France one month earlier gives a good account of how much he masters both physical performance and mental stamina.

A rainy mountaintop finish is a nightmare for a journalist. Riders end up exhausted and yearn for warm clothes and a dry shelter for their fatigued bodies – that means rapidly taking off to their buses, so few or no interviews are given out. It was a bit frustrating for me to stand at the door of the anti-doping control hoping for someone to come out of it in the mood for an interview. Only Franco Pellizotti, Vincenzo Nibali's Bahrain-Merida teammate, did.

The walk back to the press room, three kilometres under the rain, promised to be miserable, and I was rather cold despite my (amazing)

Rapha jacket. It duly began with an awful incident. I arrived at the finish line at the same time as Jelle Wallays crossed it. I could tell that, being a tall *rouleur* and having suffered several crashes, the Lotto-Soudal rider had struggled. He stopped just beyond the line and held the barriers. Then a team car screamed to a halt beside him, someone opened its back door and it slammed into Wallays' chest. He screamed and collapsed, as if he had suffered a heart attack. After several minutes of attention from the paramedics, he climbed back on his bike and soft-pedalled to the team bus, first sobbing and later outright crying. It all was incredibly sad to watch. As for my walk: I was saved by Xabier Artetxe, current Team Sky coach, who I have been friends with since his days as a DS at Caja Rural, who offered me a lift.

With the podcast in the can, we jumped back in the car and headed down to the coast. It was a special drive for me as it took me back to my home. After two weeks of La Vuelta, being able to spend a day at my parents' house in Penny Lane was something really special for me, as was showing Rich the streets where I was born and raised selling shoes, jumping fences and throwing stones at dogs to see what happened next. My whole family met for dinner and my mother prepared her delightful Spanish omelette. The combination of the tiredness of two straight days working, little sleep and the warmth of my home made me crash only ten minutes after eating.

Thursday, 31 August

Stage 12: Motril–Antequera 160.1 km
Stage winner: Tomasz Marczyński
Red jersey: Chris Froome

On Thursday I woke up at 6am and started work while my mother ironed all my clothes and we listened to the new album of my best friends' band. Spending those few hours with my family was life at its best.

Back to reality. The start town was Motril, a fishing village with a really distinctive accent. To give you a hint of how particular it is: a video of someone dubbing twenty minutes of *Pulp Fiction* with the accent went viral at the end of the noughties and is still dearly remembered all over Spain. Some of my training buddies gave me a lift to Motril, as one of them was a VIP guest of the Trek-Segafredo team and five others were tagging along hoping for a selfie with Alberto Contador. It was refreshing to share time with them, not only because they are my friends, but also because it gave me the sense of how exciting it can be for a cycling fan to be so close to the riders. 'Best birthday ever', wrote one of my pals as a caption for the picture of the whole gang with 'El Pistolero'.

That day an arsonist set fire to the Aqua Blue Sport team bus. Some guy had spent three hours setting fire to various vehicles and the small Irish team were simply unlucky to be among his victims. It was good to see the empathy and the solidarity from the rest of the race convoy. The organisers got them a bus from Bernardo, a well-known company in Almería. Every time I went on a school trip we would jump on a Bernardo bus. A couple of days later, Bernardo's coach was gone, replaced by the bus belonging to the Portuguese team LA-Aluminos.

As for the stage, the winner, Tomasz Marczyński, is one of the brightest characters in the peloton. After years struggling in the lower tiers, he has made it to the World Tour and, instead of obsessing with performance, he has vowed to enjoy his bike and to enjoy life. Seeing him winning was like a confirmation that opting for a different, laid-back approach is rewarding as long as you invest positive energy and remain committed to what you do and who you want to be.

After posing with my training buddies, Contador spent 140km in the peloton and then attacked all out up the Alto del Torcal. It was a classic Pistolero show, well supported on this occasion by his teammate Edward Theuns. It might have seemed a meaningless move had it not been for Froome's crash, which made the finale an intense chase between three groups. You could argue that the success of Contador's offensive was a matter of luck. I would say it was way more than that: that the energy he invests and the agitation he produces has an impact on the race and on his rivals.

Later that evening I reunited with Víctor for the first time in a couple of days. As we headed back to his home in Torre del Mar, a gorgeous village on the east of the Málaga province, we decided to swing by some old roads and look for a restaurant he knew near the Pantano del Agujero, one of the many water reservoirs built during Franco's dictatorship at the cost of flooding a valley, forcing the inhabitants of all the villages there to relocate to other towns. Half a century later, these 'pantanos' offer beautiful landscapes and have become sanctuaries for wildlife. Having dinner there felt somehow perfect. Again, life at its best.

Friday, 1 September

Stage 13: Coín–Tomares, 198.4km
Stage winner: Matteo Trentin
Red jersey: Chris Froome

On Thursday night, Víctor and I worked together in the small hours. We listened to my *Kilometre 0* on Sierra Nevada that was due to be released the following day. To put it together I had carried out six interviews and climbed Haza Llanas and Sierra Nevada all the way to La Hoya de la Mora – twice. That was great for my confidence as a cyclist, as it was really demanding to spend three consecutive hours climbing while thinking of smart things to say and recording them with my panting voice. But neither Víctor nor I liked the result of my effort. We found my audio pointless, but nothing could be done to fix it. *Alea jacta est*: the *Kilometre 0* came out and the feedback was reasonably good. Thank you for your kindness, dear listeners, and thanks to the producers for adding their magic.

On every stage race there is one trap-depart: that is, a start town that, thanks to the traffic and roads, proves impossible to enter, or to leave. On this Vuelta, the trap-depart was Coín. It took us an hour to get out of this beautiful village and on our way to Tomares, a town on the outskirts of Sevilla. We made it to the press room very late, and of course there was no buffet left. We were feeling unlucky until we learnt that Daniel had punctured again. That helped put things in perspective.

An uphill sprint finish was expected in Tomares and the locals in Trebujena were excited about it. This pretty town, 7,000-people strong, is deeply invested in cycling because of a local hero by the name of Juan José Lobato, a fast rider who's keen on sharp climbs, and who made his name racing for Euskaltel-Euskadi and Movistar and is now part of the LottoNL-Jumbo outfit.

Trebujeneros follow Lobato to almost every race: two buses travelled 1,800km to Paris just to watch him finish his maiden Tour de France in 2013. Fast forward to 1 September, 2017: Lobato having the chance of getting his first Grand Tour victory roughly a one-hour-drive from Trebujena was a big deal. A hopeful crowd stood a hundred metres after the finish line in LottoNL-Jumbo lookalike T-shirts, waiting for their hero to triumph. Unfortunately, he came in fifty-first. 'I have diarrhoea,' he whispered to me as he pedalled to the team bus. It was the *coup de grâce* at the end of a disappointing season, full of problems on and off the bike.

Víctor wanted to spend the night with his wife, so I booked myself a room with the podcast crew in a hotel in Triana, the authentic neighbourhood of Sevilla. We tried to have dinner at a bar that was well ranked on TripAdvisor, but instead had to settle for a random crib that turned out to be brilliant. We emptied several bottles of wine and had delightful tapas to accompany them. At some point during the dinner I had what Spanish writer Juan José Millás calls a 'reality stroke'. That is: suddenly stepping back from the moment to analyse it and realise what you are in the middle of. I found myself having dinner with some of my journalistic idols, writers whose work I had been reading for ages, sometimes even with awe. I felt really lucky, and honoured. At my best.

Saturday, 2 September

Stage 14: Écija–Sierra de la Pandera, 175km
Stage winner: Rafal Majka
Red jersey: Chris Froome

Daniel praised Andalusia on the podcast for being stunningly beautiful. He is right: this region is gorgeous for a number of reasons. It has been under the rule of different civilisations, which makes its architecture quite eclectic. There are a wide range of landscapes: the vast lowlands and the beautiful mountains; the warm, calm Mediterranean beaches; the cold, restless Atlantic ones. But bear in mind this is also one of the poorest regions. When education and industry were developed elsewhere in Spain, the majority of the land was owned by despot-like overlords that kept the population of Andalusia ignorant and struggling to survive. The empowerment of the working classes has taken place only in the last forty years or so. Perhaps in a way this has helped preserve the essence of this amazing chunk of land and its people.

Daniel is not alone in this feeling of amazement. Even though I've lived my whole life in Andalusia, I still love to contemplate it. And that is the reason why, that morning in Triana, I decided to skip my planned haircut and spent an hour sitting on a terrace instead, having breakfast and watching life happen around me.

Making it atop the Sierra de la Pandera proved to be quite difficult. Richard and I departed late from Écija as I was chatting with the president of the Spanish CPA*, then kind of messed up with the times on the roadbook – OK, we stopped too long for lunch – and made it to the climb way too late. We parked two kilometres or so from the bottom and began walking, hoping for the best. And the best happened:

* Essentially, the riders' union.

some vehicles were stuck in the road, so there was a jam that blocked
Daniel and enabled us to jump in his puncture-prone car. That saved us
a very long uphill walk.

In the confusion, I forgot to put on my decent trousers and went to
the summit of the Sierra de la Pandera with the sports shorts I usually
wore for driving (and running). Mr Richard Moore, in a low blow that
should have been sanctioned by the race jury, took a picture of me
changing out of my shorts and released it on Twitter.

Fran putting his trousers on

Reactions were mixed, and for that reason I decided the following
day to wear the most controversial piece of clothing from my wardrobe:
some shorts I bought in Hainan, with a white background decorated
with pictures of different birds. 'That will show them,' I thought. But it
only showed me.

Sunday, 3 September

Stage 15: Alcalá la Real–Sierra Nevada, 129.4km
Stage winner: Miguel Ángel López
Red jersey: Chris Froome

After a night out in my home city, with friends from the Vuelta and from the Masters course I completed last year, the big day was here: the stage to Sierra Nevada, the one I clapped my hands at enthusiastically when it was revealed in Madrid back in January.

As an amateur cyclist, it feels great to see a professional race using your training routes even if it means dropping about a hundred positions in the Strava rankings. I was particularly excited about the road to Güejar Sierra, basically the build up to Haza Llanas: I've ridden that climb more than seventy times in the three years I've been living in Granada. I know every slight rise, every pothole, every tricky corner, and watching the pros power along that road was inspiring and humbling at the same time.

But to be honest, the stage disappointed me. I was expecting fireworks from the favourites, and they didn't come until the last kilometre except for the usual Contador show and the flight of Superman López to his second stage victory. I asked Froome in the press conference about this lack of aggression, and he told the room that the second week had been very demanding and therefore the legs were pretty tired. Fair enough.

Besides López, Ilnur Zakarin was probably the biggest winner of the day as he reasserted his candidacy for a podium spot in Madrid. I duly bide my time for half an hour standing beside the anti-doping truck to speak with him on one of our usual three- or four-way interviews. I have this situation with Zakarin: I somehow identify with him, with his way of relating to people, that shy smile and that inability to communicate with people outside his circle. Empathy between us has been growing in the last couple of years and, although we are not and will never become friends, I can feel he is comfortable speaking with me even with his doctor/masseur/press officer/roommate acting as translator.

Talking about empathy: before recording the podcast I ran into Javi Moreno, the Bahrain-Merida rider who crashed out of the Vuelta on stage 2. He came to Sierra Nevada to collect his belongings from the team bus, where they had been stuck since he was taken by an ambulance with his jaw broken and nine fewer teeth. When we spoke, his mouth was completely wired and he was still feeding himself with a straw. Barely opening his lips, he told me Bahrain was not extending his contract after his disappointing season. Knowing him and his family for a long time, and having been to his home for an interview, I couldn't help but feel for him, his wife and their two kids. Luckily, a couple of weeks later I learnt he was joining Delko-Marseille, a French professional team.

And so Richard and I proceeded to record our last podcast together, on the heights of Sierra Nevada. I was in awe looking down the valley, contemplating all the roads I usually pedal, realising how small and big everything was depending on how we looked at it. It felt like perfect closure for the second chapter of the Vuelta . . .

Later, Víctor, Richard and I had dinner together. It was a pleasant one: food was great and the conversation, too. Even if we didn't drink alcohol, we were laughing loud and, all in all, enjoying ourselves until we were the last people in the bar. When we were done eating, I raised my hand and told the waiter: 'Bring all the shots, all the desserts and the check!' It was meant to be a funny way of asking for the check but, five minutes later, he appeared with an enormous plate piled high with three pieces of every dessert they had: cheesecake, apple pie, muffins, mango ice cream . . .

Oh God! 'Man, sorry, there has been some confusion,' I told him. 'I was joking.'

'Oh,' he replied. 'You were joking? Well, I am working.'

Both my face and Víctor's turned white. We didn't want to eat that food nor pay for it – there was €40 worth of desserts on that big plate! We began whispering to each other in Spanish. How on earth could we make the waiter change his mind and take the desserts back where they belonged? And then we heard the word 'tasty' coming from Richard's corner of the table. Not realising what was going on, he had attacked the mango ice cream. That was his verdict on its flavour: 'Tasty'. Víctor and I could feel €40 slipping out of our wallet: now that Richard had touched the plate, our options of returning them without charge were even slimmer.

Fortunately, the waiter came to terms with my 'joke' and understood that, when I asked him to bring all the shots and all the desserts, I didn't mean it literally. We left him a huge tip, and Richard left us with an anecdote we told fellow Spanish journalists a hundred times and a word, 'tasty', we said during every meal of the third week.

16. END OF THE TEAM?

Joe Dombrowski

Joe Dombrowski

'Joe, how's the Vuelta?' read the WhatsApp message on my phone after stage 7 of the Vuelta. It was Andrew McQuaid, my agent. The bulk of Andrew's work comes when it's time for me to negotiate a new contract, but he keeps tabs on things throughout the year, and checking in mid-Grand Tour was nothing out of the ordinary. I replied saying I didn't seem to be riding great, but things were OK otherwise, and I asked how he was doing.

'Bad news,' he replied. 'Your team might be folding next year.'

Not exactly what I wanted to hear near the end of the year with seemingly very average form. Jonathan Vaughters, our team manager, had contacted Andrew that morning letting him know of an unexpected budget shortfall. There weren't many details, but it sounded like a budget that seemed secure for 2018, was actually riding on a not totally secure sponsorship deal after the Tour de France, and when it came down to the final board meeting, one guy voted against it, and that was that.

At that point, I was the only one at the Vuelta who knew about our situation. I sat silently on the transfer to the hotel wondering when the news would break with the team. I overheard Simon Clarke lamenting the fact that he hadn't signed yet for 2018. He was concerned because he had never signed a contract this late before, and the team had gone silent. It was killing me to not say anything. Morally, I felt obliged to tell him that he best get looking around, and quickly. It felt wrong to be privy to this sort of information and to keep it to myself, while it seemed that so many people's livelihoods were going to be at risk.

I was roommates with Mike Woods. He was enjoying some fantastic form. The best of his career. He was out of contract for 2018, and he was in a great position to negotiate with teams – his stock was rising. Mike and I get along well, and he was bouncing his thoughts off me as he worked through his contract negotiations. Mike was constantly on the phone with his agent, fielding queries from teams. We were pretty open with sharing news. We had just arrived at our hotel room after stage 7, and Mike was again on the phone with his agent. He put the phone aside as we walked in, and told his agent he'd call him straight back after he stepped outside. Clearly they had to talk about something they didn't want me to know, though I had a pretty good idea.

Mike came back into the room and sat down on his bed. I looked over to him and said, 'I was going to tell you something, but I have a feeling you might know.' He looked at me with a nervous sort of half-smile. 'You got the news too?' We made an agreement of sorts to keep it between us for a day. Surely the team would be letting riders know shortly, and if not, since rider agents had already been notified, the news would spread like wildfire.

Enjoying a joke on the team bus

Riders and staff of the Slipstream Sports family —
Confidential
We are surprised and saddened to write you this note. Our team's chances of securing a UCI license for 2018 are now very uncertain.

Yesterday we were given some shocking news about a new partner we were relying on. Unfortunately, a last minute board of directors decision turned against us. Without their support we cannot guarantee financial security in 2018. More specifically, we cannot guarantee we will be able to acquire a World Tour license and to meet the financial criteria required by the UCI. This situation may resolve in our favor in the next days – and we may find new financial backing. However, since we cannot guarantee you that, as of today, we need to be forthright and let all of you look for your best options. Slipstream Sports will continue to fight to continue in 2018, but it's time to let all of you know our future is not guaranteed.

As of Monday, Aug. 21 all staff of Slipstream Sports are released from any and all contractual obligations for 2018 and beyond and are free to pursue other opportunities.

We need to clarify that all of our current sponsors and partners (Cannondale, Drapac, Oath, POC) have remained committed to support our team in 2018. These sponsors have lived up to their promises. But, unfortunately, without additional financial backing, the numbers just don't add up.

We are still working to keep this team alive because we believe in its ethos and because we believe in all of you. We have several opportunities that may come through. In the past, other teams have found support quite late in the season. However, we're simply not comfortable exposing all of you to the uncertainties of Slipstream's future any longer.

We are unspeakably sorry to deliver this message. We hope we can ride together in 2018 and beyond. Thank you for your dedication to the team and your sacrifices over the years to keep us on the road.

—Doug & JV

I received this email the following day and read it after the stage. I was one of the last riders back to the bus that day, and I knew that the news had arrived when I stepped on and the usual endorphin-fuelled fury of post-stage anecdotes were replaced by an unusually sombre mood. All the riders were sat in their seats, glued to their phones. I was expecting it, so I suppose it softened the blow, but the others had no idea. There were a few murmurs in the bunch that day, but before that email, you optimistically ignore and deflect any comments. Simon Clarke was asked by another rider if he was going to be OK before he even received the email. It never would have taken long – JV tells the agents to start looking around, the agents talk to other team managers, and in a somewhat twisted way other teams probably see some great assets soon to be floating around at bargain basement prices. People talk.

The transfer after that stage was the quietest bus ride I've ever taken.

When there was conversation it always swirled around 'what ifs' and optimistic speculation, but it was ultimately cloaked in the grim reality that if the team did not find a sponsor, for what was purportedly a $7-million budget shortfall, in the next two weeks, then the team would fold. We had until about the end of the Vuelta. There was never a defined window, but that's what seemed realistic. Rigoberto Urán came forward and said he would give the team two weeks to find a solution. It was a generous offer, but at the same time I saw through to the harsh reality. Late in the year, after having signed a very sizeable contract, Rigo would have potentially been a significantly cheaper signing if the team folded. He wanted to see everyone around next year, but I'm sure he didn't want to take a pay cut either. He had just finished second in the Tour de France. Finding a job wouldn't have been an issue, but a pay cut on his freshly inked contract probably would have. That trickle-down effect for the rest of us would have been the reality. Take a spot wherever you can, for whatever money you can, and just be happy you weren't one of the guys to miss out in the game of musical chairs.

The team meeting on the bus the day after the news was the shortest meeting of the Vuelta, but by far the most emotional. I'm not a particularly emotional sort of guy, but I remember looking down at my seat so as not to make eye contact with anyone. Our director Juan Manuel (JuanMa) Gárate stood at the front of the bus and gave us two options. Option 1 – Some of us have families, wives, and kids to support and houses to pay for. We can all ride for our own results, as individuals, and no one will have a problem with that. Option 2 – We will ride as a team, commit to the best possible result, and race to win. We voted by a show of hands. Everyone raised their hands for option 2.

'OK, guys, today we will ride for Mike,' JuanMa told us. 'We will control the race from kilometre zero, until the final climb, and we will race to win the stage with Mike. You are professionals, you know what to do.' The meeting was so short, it felt like an eternity before the start, and journalists were crowded outside the bus. I jokingly offered to sell interviews for a nominal fee of $7 million. We all laughed, but only half-heartedly.

That stage was one of the most cohesive, concerted efforts I have ever seen from our team. It's perhaps something we've lacked in the past. A team of many strong individuals, there or thereabouts, but lacking unity and wins. Everyone was committed. We rode from start to finish. Mike finished third behind Chris Froome and Esteban Chaves. A great result. Froome commended our efforts after the stage, admiring our strength and team ethic in the face of such an adverse scenario.

The amount of speculation about our prospects in the latter half of the Vuelta was unbelievable. John Murray is a British *soigneur* who works for our team. I saw him for a massage after every stage and the first words he asked me when I walked into his room each evening were simply 'Any news?', hoping that I had some morsel of information that the others didn't. I can understand public apathy towards the plight of professional – highly paid, self-centred – athletes. Thing is, a World Tour team can be close to a hundred people across the organisation. Staff – mechanics, *soigneurs*, physios, doctors and other medical staff – are on one-year contracts, and often fairly modest salaries. Just as the rider market would be flooded in the event of the team's collapse, the number of staff looking for a job would far outnumber the available spots.

Dinner table chatter and post-race transfer discussions centred around a lot of what ifs, and any time any news became available it offered a new titbit to dissect. When the team announced it would attempt to close the budget shortfall via crowdfunding it was a topic of great debate, but it made me even more pessimistic. A professional sports team funded via fans? Really? I mean, from the optimist's point of view we could point to other sports that essentially pull funds from fans. Stadium sports sell tickets to gain entry and see the live event. Boxing sells fights to pay-per-view television, and can generate $200 million for a major fight. Hell, the American football team the Green Bay Packers have sold shares in the team dating back to 1923 on a number of occasions. The most recent offering was to raise money for a stadium expansion in 2011, and $64 million had been raised by the year's end. A hefty sum, considering that your $250 share price would pay no dividends, would not appreciate in financial terms, was not tradeable on any sort of market, and didn't have the protection of any security you'd purchase under normal investment conditions. Despite all the drawbacks, Packers fans flock to become an 'owner' of the team. Even looking through the lens of other sports, the bottom line is, this is cycling. We can't contain fans in a stadium for live spectating like basketball, we don't sell TV rights like boxing (we don't even own them), and I just am not sure cycling has the fan base like American football that you would raise those sort of funds from your fans.

Our team at the Vuelta remained incredibly focused on the race given the circumstances, but any spare time was occupied pontificating doubt or optimism when the reality is that no one had any real idea. A week after the announcement we received another email from Vaughters.

Everyone:
No promises. No assurances. However, we may have some good news for everyone in the coming week.
This isn't a done deal, not by a long stretch. But there is reason for optimism.
Keep the faith.
Thank you all. JV.

In truth, the email meant about as much as my contract at that point. They could inspire positivity, but both were essentially meaningless. Regardless, my attitude from that point forward took a swing toward cautious optimism.

Each day after the ambiguous message from JV, I was getting snippets of information from Mike Woods and Simon Clarke and the possibility of JV's email carrying real weight seemed a little better. Another week passed before we received another email from the boss just three days before the end of the Vuelta.

> *Everyone:*
> *As of right now, I am informing you that if you have a contract with*
> *Slipstreamsports for 2018, we are enforcing your contract.*
> *More to come.*
> *Thank you all. JV*

We still hadn't received any official information from the team regarding how the budget shortfall was closed, but despite the sparse update, the feeling of elation across the team was palpable. There were hugs, and high-fives, and smiles all around.

It was later revealed that the new sponsor was EF Education First, a Boston-based education company with a focus on international programmes and languages. They seemed a good fit for a professional cycling team. Cyclists can be great ambassadors for speaking foreign languages, and the education aspect meshed well with the team's ethos. Michael Drapac, one of the team's owners, has a vision to create a holistic environment for us, where we can plan for life after cycling. That idea seemed all the more important after the situation we found ourselves in the two weeks prior.

Despite the feeling of relief, I knew we had dodged a bullet. As I discussed the news with my agent I joked that JV was like a cockroach. A pro-cycling survivalist. Nothing can kill him. This wasn't the first time our team had been in a tough spot financially, but Vaughters has managed to keep the ship afloat on each occasion. The unfortunate truth is that this problem is not unique to our team. The scare we experienced during the Vuelta is commonplace in the world of professional cycling and it is the manifestation of the broken model that professional cycling operates on. Of course I was happy our team would continue, but the past two weeks made me more pessimistic and cynical about the health of the sport. This scenario seems to happen to one or two World Tour teams every year and risks putting a huge number of riders and staff out of a job.

Chris Froome dominated the Vuelta. He was incredibly strong in his own right, but his support from Team Sky, the wealthiest team in the World Tour, was equally impressive. Froome's dominance combined with the news of our team's situation sparked debate in the media as to whether cycling would be better with salary caps. Even Alberto Contador, in his final race as a professional, weighed in: he was in favour.

From a myopic viewpoint, I would echo Contador's sentiment. Sky dominates Grand Tour racing. Frankly, the Tour de France nowadays can be a bit boring. In response to the suggestions of salary caps, Froome said, 'If you take that away, what do teams have to strive for? Why are you working harder? To win more races. To take that away, it's almost as if we are becoming communists.' He continued: 'We should all ride the same bikes. We should all have the same equipment sponsors. We should eat the same rice and porridge each morning. Where do you draw the line?' Much has been made of Team Sky's implementation of 'marginal gains'. Their approach and attention to detail has been credited for their success. Having ridden for both Team Sky and Cannondale, I can attest to the vast support network at Sky, but I also feel that their success is largely on account of their payroll. Bluntly, Sky has the most money, and the best riders follow the best money. Therefore, Sky has the best riders.

I signed for Sky as a neo-pro. I went because they seemed to have the best support, but I also went because they paid me the most money. I was very successful in the amateur ranks and I had my pick of teams to choose from for my first professional contract. It goes back to the best riders following the best money.

In American football, the teams get a draft pick for players coming out of college. The worst teams, organised by their previous season's record, get the first picks. It's an effort to level the playing field. In European football, transfer fees are paid from new team to old for the 'development' of the acquired player. If cycling drew from these sorts of models, perhaps I would have started out at a 'poor team' like Cannondale as a neo-pro, developed as a rider, and gone to Team Sky with Cannondale receiving a 'development fee' from my future employer. Instead things panned out the opposite. The model of cycling encourages that scenario, and it becomes a race to the bottom for the teams with lower budgets. From a racing standpoint, less competition is just plain less interesting to watch. Economically speaking, it puts lower budget teams on the ropes, and every year the scenario my team found itself in repeats.

I mentioned earlier that I was in favour of salary caps from a 'myopic' viewpoint. The other issue with great budget disparities between teams is that the level of investment required to field a competitive team is always a race to chase the budgets of the teams at the top. Cycling does not currently generate revenue outside of sponsorship and that is the key issue. When a team like Sky has a budget double that of other teams in the World Tour, the amount of money a team manager is looking for from potential sponsors is often beyond what those potential sponsors are willing to fork out. The budget of a team like Sky creates a price floor of sorts above the equilibrium market price, and the surplus that is created essentially manifests itself in the form of teams in danger of folding each season. It's a similar scenario to government-imposed minimum wages. The government regulates minimum wage with a price floor. That number is set to benefit the liveability of the minimum wage earner while not being set so high that unskilled labour sees a spike in unemployment rates due to the wage being well above the equilibrium market price. In professional cycling, teams such as Sky at the top of the budget pyramid act as the 'government' in that sense. The problem is the 'price floor' is set too high. Salary caps could work to distribute budgets more evenly across teams and lower the entry price for potential sponsors wanting to come into the cycling market.

To all the riders baulking at the idea of a smaller paycheque, I see another scenario. Salary caps could offer a more secure model. The rider market is at risk of being flooded every year by teams that collapse, devaluing contracts. Talent would be more evenly distributed across teams, and if anything, I think a more stable team environment would ease shocks to the rider market preventing lean years. In my short-sighted, myopic, view of the current cycling landscape, I do think that salary caps would be a step in the right direction, but again, the real issue with our sport is that we are dependent upon sponsorship revenue to operate. I don't believe we will see salaries similar to other sports until that changes, and in the immediate future the lack of regulation of that market kills the sport from within.

In the long term, I would like to see professional cycling own what it produces. The Tour de France is the best attended sporting event in the world, and it is in the top five most watched sporting events in the world. Despite the popularity of the world's biggest bike race, we have yet to figure out how to monetise our own participation. Rather than turning a profit across multiple revenue streams from being the star act in one of the world's iconic sporting events, we fight each other in an under-regulated market for advertising space on clothing and buses. In my mind, we are all missing the bigger picture here. More money in the sport is appealing, but really I would be happy with a bit more stability. As it stands now, our own model is responsible for the turbulent job market in which we suffer. After the 2017 Vuelta I can get behind a more stable environment.

I hope my co-workers can too.

17. VUELTA A ESPAÑA DIARY: WEEK 3

Lionel Birnie

Monday, 4 September

Stung by the outrageous suggestion that I had treated my first stint at the Vuelta like a holiday, I resolve to at least have a look at the general classification on the flight to Bilbao to remind myself what's been going on. Nothing much appears to have changed since I was last there. A chap called Froome is still leading.

I am joking, of course. During my week at home, I had watched most of the stages on television and on the days I missed the race live I had managed to piece together what had happened with some degree of accuracy by listening to Richard's erratic interpretation of the daily Tale of the Etapa on the podcast.

My travelling companion for the week, Simon, volunteers to drive our hire car from Bilbao to Logroño. As the Fiat 500L labours up the first gentle incline on our exit from the airport car park, I wonder how it will cope with the 20 per cent sections of the Angliru and resolve to make that not my problem by engineering things so that Simon drives that day.

It doesn't take me long to get into the Holiday Grand Tour vibe because I promptly fall asleep in the passenger seat and wake only when we reach the outskirts of Logroño, the largest town in the Rioja region. There's no time for a glass of rich, oaky red wine yet, though, because there's work to be done. We head across town for Chris Froome's rest-day press conference, which takes place in the glamorous reception-slash-breakfast room of Team Sky's hotel.

As the low-key gathering breaks up, a couple of colleagues speculate that Froome sounded a bit chesty and was stifling the urge to cough, as if he might have a cold coming on. I nod sagely in agreement while thinking that he sounded fine to me. I think they're hoping for something to loosen Froome's grip on the lead to lend a bit of drama to the race in the final week.

Simon and I head into Logroño for a pre-dinner drink. 'I hope we haven't missed happy hour,' I say. We settle on a busy bar in the square opposite the cathedral. My heart sinks when the waiter realises we are British and declares he has just the thing for us. He returns with two half-litres of industrial-strength lager. Does he mistake me for a British holidaymaker who got lost on the way to Benidorm? I take a sip and try to disguise a wince as the metallic tang tweaks my taste buds.

Despite this, I ask him to recommend a restaurant and he points us in the direction of a narrow side street lined on both sides with small, bustling tapas bars. There's something strangely intimidating about how

A pre-dinner drink in Logroño

informal and relaxed it all is. People stand at tables made from large oak barrels, or sit on stools at the bar. The menus are either exhaustive or non-existent. It's the sort of casual dining we're not terribly good at in Britain and so Simon and I find ourselves walking up and down the street unable to decide which place to enter.

Then I spot two amigos from the press room – Andy Hood and Pete Cossins. Hoody has lived in Léon in north-western Spain for years and Pete spent some time in Valencia when he was younger, so I assume they know the ropes.

'How does this all work?' I ask.

'You just order what you want,' says Hoody, who approaches the counter and makes a series of vague hand gestures and then tells me food and wine are coming. It's as easy as that when you know the language and the customs.

We stand and eat, drink and chat about the race. As the wine takes over, I set out on a half-baked theory about Chris Froome's Grand Tour strategy this summer, drawing a comparison with the board game, Monopoly. As I get underway, I become acutely aware that I've not quite thought the analogy through and don't know how it finishes. I frequently feel like this when recording the podcast.

'Froome rode the Tour conservatively and without being flash,' I say. 'He bought the four railway stations, the Water Works and the Electric Company and quietly did enough to win the game.' Hoody and Pete don't laugh or shoot me down in flames. Another sip of wine encourages me to push on. 'But here at the Vuelta, he made a big move early and snapped up Mayfair and Park Lane, the most prestigious properties on the board, then he added houses and hotels as and when he could, knowing that he could sit back and watch the rent roll in during the final stages of the game.'

It's gone reasonably well, so I make a mental note to give it an airing in the podcast. Before I ask which counter Froome would choose if he were to play a game of Monopoly (it would definitely be the top hat) we head off to another bar for a nightcap.

It's just after midnight – early for Spain – and as we sit down the Vuelta's young workforce arrive dressed up in their best clothes. (That is to say, not a polo shirt with a Vuelta a España logo on it and shorts.) A group of them wander off, presumably in search of a better party, but they return a few minutes later meaning this must be the best Logroño has to offer. The Vuelta rest day party is just about getting started but it's past my bed time and as we're not here on holiday Simon and I head back to our hotel with the beginnings of a Rioja headache tapping at our skulls.

Tuesday, 5 September

Stage 16: Circuito de Navarra–Logroño, 40.2km
Stage winner: Chris Froome
Red jersey: Chris Froome

Team Sky's 'modest' race hub

The Vuelta resumes with a time trial starting at a motor racing circuit in the middle of nowhere. The team buses are parked in a line next to the pit lane and there's something quite symbolic about the fact that Aqua Blue and Team Sky are at polar opposite ends. Aqua Blue, the Irish wild-card outfit, has been lent a bus by a Portuguese team after their own was destroyed by an arsonist in Almería. At the other end, Team Sky have their two-storey 'race hub', which must have cost about the same as a decent GC contender and has been folded out like something from the Transformers movie.

I wait to speak to Lachlan Morton, one of only three Dimension Data riders to have made it this far, and I'm shown onto the bus to find him wriggling into his aerodynamic overshoes like a diver putting on a wetsuit. This is Morton's first Grand Tour, and it's not quite turned out the way he expected. Illness and crashes have knocked the team's riders out one by one leaving just him, Igor Antón and Jacques Janse van Rensburg to start the final week. Morton's looking on the bright side, though. 'Bike riders generally are so worried about themselves they just see the positives. People have been saying to me, "you must have so much room on the bus", but really I'd much rather have less space and still have nine guys.'

I see Hoody and I tell him I've just spoken to Morton.

'Ah man,' he says, 'did you use the hand gel afterwards?'

'No,' I say.

'Their whole team has been sick. Earlier in the race I interviewed one of their guys and I swear that night I was shitting through the eye of a needle.'

Only when it's time to head to Logroño do Simon and I realise that the only route we can take is along the course, following one of the riders. We sit on the motor racing circuit's start grid in our Fiat 500L waiting for Aldemar Reyes of the Manzana-Postobon team to roll down the ramp. A Vuelta official waves us off and Simon has the Fiat in the red before we reach the first chicane.

We settle in behind Reyes and enjoy the ride. It's not long before we can see his teammate, Ricardo Vilela, who set off a minute behind him, in our rear-view mirrors. Simon hugs the right-hand side of the road, two tyres on the dusty verge, to give Vilela space but he's using us as a wind shield and he passes impressively, if terrifyingly, close. His teammate Reyes gets on Vilela's wheel and for a long while there's a Manzana-Postobon two-up time trial going on, which the *commissaires* might take a dim view of if they see it.

Then Quick-Step's Bob Jungels comes flying past at such speed that I am convinced he's in contention for the stage victory. It surprises me when I see the results later to find he finished only twelfth, two minutes slower than Froome.

As exhilarating as it was to drive in the thick of the action, it's a relief to get our car to the finish and out of the way of the cyclists and their spindly limbs. Simon's driving was immaculate and yet all I could think of was the headlines if anything went wrong: 'Idiots ruin time trial.'

After a long drive we meet up with Daniel and his ITV cameraman, Scott, for a disappointing dinner. The hake is so mushy and watery I would bet it had been defrosted in a microwave. It's covered in a tasteless white sauce which serves only to make it harder to pick out the bones, of which there are many. I make a note to have a word with the holiday rep about the standard of catering.

Wednesday, 6 September

Stage 17: Villadiego–Los Machucos, 180.5km
Stage winner: Stefan Denifl
Red jersey: Chris Froome

Only cars with a special sticker will be allowed to drive to the top of the Alto de Los Machucos and only cars with four occupants will be given a sticker by the Vuelta organisers, so our Fiat is spared the humiliation of grinding to a halt on the steep slopes of the Vuelta's recently discovered gem.

We arrange to follow Daniel and Scott to the bottom of the climb, ditch our car in a village trusting that the Vuelta press stickers will ensure it's still there when we return, and climb in with them.

Scott pulls away and as we turn the corner the road narrows and steepens dramatically, causing the car to rev loudly enough that the people walking up the hill turn to look. We stall and roll backwards. Now the engine is silent we can hear the laughter.

'Do you fancy taking over?' Scott asks Daniel.

'Not really,' says Daniel.

There's an uncomfortably long pause, which I choose to ignore by looking out of the window. There's a fascinating dry-stone wall to my left and I'm struck by the way the bricks have been arranged. It really is quite special.

'I'll have a go,' says Simon, at last.

It's a hairy drive. The engine screams and the wheels spin as we crawl forward and the gradient is such that there's the ever-present fear of stalling and not getting going again.

Potential headlines are scrolling through my mind again: 'Idiots ruin mountain stage.'

The road is spectacular. Parts of it are rough and cracked. It's damp in places and sheltered by trees. Then there's a sudden steep downhill part that comes out of nowhere and sends us plummeting like a runaway car on a rollercoaster. Later there's a section of ridged concrete panels that might offer enough grip to at least allow the riders to get out of the saddle without their rear wheels spinning.

We make it to the top in time to watch a thrilling pursuit match between Stefan Denifl of Aqua Blue and Alberto Contador, riding his final Grand Tour. Denifl hangs on a lot more comfortably than might have been expected.

Rick Delaney, the team's Monaco-based millionaire owner, celebrates like a prog-rocker whose album has just gone platinum. The minutes

Stefan Denifl keeping Contador at arm's length

tick on and as the other Aqua Blue riders cross the line they gather next to the podium to share the moment. How will they celebrate tonight? I ask Lasse Norman Hansen. 'We have a no-alcohol rule during races,' he says, 'but I think tonight we can have a glass of something.'

As we descend in the car I ponder the idea of *The Cycling Podcast* imposing a no-alcohol rule at races. I doubt I'd make the first rest day.

Thursday, 7 September

Stage 18: Suances–Santo Toribio de Liébana, 169km
Stage winner: Sander Armée
Red jersey: Chris Froome

Our hotel is within walking distance of where the stage starts in Suances. We'd arrived after dark the previous evening so I hadn't appreciated what a pretty little seaside town it is. One of the jewels in Cantabria's tourism crown, apparently.

I head to Quick-Step's bus and wait for their Italian *rouleur*-sprinter, Matteo Trentin, who has three stage wins to his name already (and will win a fourth in Madrid). I ask him who would win a three-up sprint between him and his two Quick-Step teammates – Fernando Gaviria, who won four stages of the Giro, and Marcel Kittel, who won five at the Tour.

'Depends,' he says. 'In a straight line, Kittel. In a twisty finish, Gaviria. With me always being second or third.' He laughs self-deprecatingly and, after I've turned off the recorder, adds, 'I guess next year we might find out?' In 2018, they will all be in different teams, with Kittel joining Katusha-Alpecin and Trentin heading to Orica.

Unless you are Lotto-Soudal's *domestique* Sander Armée, who outmanoeuvres Alexey Lutsenko to win the stage, it proves to be a fairly uneventful day.* Fran and I record the podcast outside a bar in the little town of Potes, knowing we each have a long drive ahead of us.

'Tonight's hotel could be a bit of a wild card,' says Simon as we pull away. It turns out to be the biggest understatement of the Vuelta since 'Team Sky look quite strong.'

There's a three-hour drive up over two first-category climbs. The first takes us above the clouds but by the time we reach the second it's dark and our eyes are playing tricks on us. Our car's headlights are reflected back at us by pairs of eyes on the roadside. At one point, what appears to be a goat runs out in front of us and takes us all the way across the

---

* Ha! With hindsight, it might prove to have been the most eventful day of the 2017 Vuelta, since it was after this stage that Chris Froome's urine sample contained an excess of salbutamol, the asthma drug that is permitted to a certain threshold. This is known as an adverse analytical finding rather than a positive test. At the time of writing the case remains unresolved. It could end up with Froome suspended and stripped of his Vuelta title. Or it might not. I don't like speculation at the best of times, but this is particularly exasperating.

road like a sprinter with scant regard for niceties such as holding his line.

We head deeper into the Cantabrian mountains, following Google Maps on my phone. The owner of the guest house we're heading to has sent Simon an email with directions. It reads, 'Turn left at the bridge of trolls.'

With each turn the road gets narrower until finally we are on what looks like the Alto de Los Machucos – a steep, ridged concrete path leading to a rough track. Finally, we see two parked cars and lights coming from a house up the hill.

'Here we are,' says Simon, confidently.

I send him off to check we're in the right place and as soon as he gets out of the car, dogs start barking. This sets off wilder, more distant-sounding dogs in the hills. I decide to wait in the car.

Simon returns, with our host. He has an unsmiling face. I do a half-turn and almost fall into a huge dog that has silently settled by my side. All that's missing is the comedy sound effect of a crack of thunder.

Once in the light of the house, Señor's face is as cold and unwelcoming as I feared. He shows us upstairs to our rooms and I am struck by the cold smell of damp stone. He has no English, we have no Spanish, so we're finding it tricky to warm things up. He uses the international sign language for 'food', which is generous of him because it's very late. I smile and give the thumbs-up and for the first time he appears to be not terrifying.

After he's gone downstairs, I open the door to my room and as soon as I turn on the light a black shape flutters rapidly across the ceiling, then round and round in demented circles.

'Simon, there's a bat in my room!'

Simon finds this hilarious for two reasons. Firstly, this week's five-minute internet sensation is a video of an Irish family trying to shoo a bat out of their kitchen, and secondly, this is the very week my Irish citizenship application has been accepted. The coincidence is too much and between fits of laughter, Simon mimics the Irishman in the bat video.

'Get it, Lionel. Get it.'

Simon goes downstairs and I hear him struggling to explain what's going on. Finally the penny drops and Señor guffaws. 'Ah, Batman! Yes! Na-na-na-na-na-na-na-na-Batman!'

It's hard to believe but things get weirder, although my nerves are eased a little by the fact Señor has a wife, who is friendly and speaks a bit of French. This not only makes communication easier but also allows me to believe for the first time that we will get out of here in the morning.

Using a translation website on his laptop, Señor offers us 'chickens soup' or 'meat terrine' to start, followed by 'fish of lake' or 'kid stew'. I go for the chicken and the kid, which I assume will be goat.

The chicken soup is grey and watery, with a whiff of carcass. It's not much more than stock, really, with flecks of meat floating in it. In a word, I'd describe it as challenging, but it is nothing compared to the stew, which seems to be fist-sized bones, connective tissue and meat that manages to be both tough and gelatinous at the same time. As goats go, this one definitely spent its life as a mountain *domestique*. Let's face it, no one sits down to a nice plate of Mikel Nieve, do they? I manage to eat just about enough to avoid offending our hosts.

As we eat, Señor sits at a desk with his laptop open, watching us. Only now do I realise that the song 'Hallelujah', originally by Leonard Cohen, has been playing on a loop since we arrived. There's not just the Cohen original, there's a version from what looks to be a Russian talent show, a version by a choir of children, a version by Susan Boyle. It takes me a while to work out that Señor is playing them from his laptop via a big television screen on the wall behind him.

'I think he quite likes this song,' I say to Simon between mouthfuls of gristle.

The music stops, which makes me look up at the screen. I do a double-take because there's Señor, dressed like a sort of Spanish Ray

Mears, in khakis and a wide-brimmed hat, which I now notice takes pride of place resting on a glass skull on the mantelpiece.

With the aid of his laptop and the translation website he manages to explain that he's an expert not only in survival techniques but also the natural world and that the film we're watching is from a television programme about Cantabrian wildlife he made about twenty years ago.

Then 'Hallelujah' kicks in yet again and we decide it's time for bed. Fortunately, the bat has made its way out through the open window while we were eating. Unfortunately, the bed sheets are cold and slightly damp.

Friday, 8 September

Stage 19: Caso–Gijón, 149.7km
Stage winner: Thomas De Gendt
Red jersey: Chris Froome

It's a big weekend in Gijón because it's Asturias Day. I ask Fran what it's in aid of and he's not quite sure. The internet tells me it's the day the locals celebrate winning the battle of Covadonga, which is either the day Pedro Delgado won a stage of the 1985 Vuelta at Lagos de Covadonga or, much more likely, the victory by a small band of Asturians who beat back a much larger army of Moorish invaders in the eighth century. It's a big sporting weekend too, because the Vuelta reaches its climax on the Angliru and Sporting Gijón meet their great rivals Real Oviedo for the first time in almost fifteen years.

Before that, there's a stage finish on the seafront in Gijón. There's a buzz of excitement when Ivan Garcia Cortina of Bahrain-Merida, who was born in the city, escapes over the final climb but at the finish everyone is left scratching their heads wondering how Nicolas Roche managed to lose out in a sprint to Thomas De Gendt and Jarlinson Pantano, and everyone else in the group.

De Gendt's victory is Lotto-Soudal's second stage win in a row. During the winter, De Gendt had told *The Cycling Podcast* that, having won a Giro stage on the great Stelvio, and a Tour stage on the giant Ventoux, he had his sights set on the Angliru. Not bad, Thomas, not bad. Only one day out.

All week, Fran has been going on about cachopo, the Asturian speciality, and so he has booked the best cachopo restaurant in Gijón for us. Cachopo is all new to me but it turns out to be a thin beef or veal steak stuffed with ham and cheese, covered in breadcrumbs and deep fried. It's served on a bed of patatas bravas, peppers and mushrooms. We order several to share and Fran asks for my verdict. I have to say it lives up to the hype. The steak is soft and tasty and the whole thing is something of a guilty pleasure, a bit like a really juicy hamburger. I'm less keen on the cider, which is another Asturian speciality. Unlike the excellent ciders in Brittany, Normandy or the West Country, for that matter, which are so pleasingly dry they force the lips to pucker up with each sip, this stuff is more like the cider that comes in two-litre bottles and is best served to teenagers in British parks. The custom of pouring it from a great height to aerate it, and serving it a little bit at a time, does nothing to improve it either.

Saturday, 9 September

Stage 20: Corvera de Asturias–Alto de l'Angliru, 117.5km
Stage winner: Alberto Contador
Red jersey: Chris Froome

A minibus has been laid on to take journalists and photographers to the top of the Angliru. It was supposed to leave at noon but it's twenty-five past and we're still waiting. Eventually we set off with a police motorcycle escort and the engine labours as soon as the road gets steep. We press on for a few kilometres and then pull over in a large layby.

Reports are of an accident further up the mountain. The air ambulance has been called and we have to wait.

Eventually, a policeman tells us the bus is going no further. He gives us three options – we can either walk back down to the press centre, stay where we are, or walk to the top, which is eight kilometres away.

Fran seems unconcerned about this but I suddenly realise I have only a light jacket and nothing to eat or drink. I'm also fifteen years older and an unspecified number of kilograms heavier than him. I decide I have to be in the early break so I set off with barely a glance over my shoulder. We may be teammates but it's every man and woman for themselves now. I leave him laughing and chatting and, I think, eating a biscuit. Apart from wishing that I also had a biscuit, I have no regrets.

I stride up a very steep section and realise it's going to take me a long time to walk to the top. Up ahead I see a woman pleading with the passing vehicles to give her a lift. She's having no luck until she decides to walk in the middle of the road, which forces the next vehicle, a small white van covered in Vuelta logos, to stop behind her. She waves her accreditation at the driver. The driver shakes his head but she's not taking no for an answer and manages to open the back door of the van before he can drive off. Noticing there's room for a not-so-small one, I get in too.

Where's Fran? Who knows? Who cares? I am Warren Barguil, he is Wilco Kelderman. I've got ages to get my story straight.

I get out of the van at the top, feeling warm and smug, only to see Fran waving from the back of an open-sided truck just behind us. He'd hitched a lift moments after me.

The race itself is the Alberto Contador Show. He wins his final mountain stage as a professional, just as everyone thought he would.

It's chaotic at the top of the Angliru after the race. Riders continue to cross the line for the best part of half-an-hour. They are directed to a marquee where they can at least change into some dry clothing before descending down the mountain again. In another tent, Froome is surrounded by cameras and microphones and I just about catch him saying that the Vuelta is his now. Steady on, Chris, there's still a circuit race in Madrid to come . . .

Sunday, 10 September

Stage 21: Arroyomolinos–Madrid, 117.6km
Stage winner: Matteo Trentin
Red jersey: Chris Froome

No Madrid for us, so we head to Asturias airport at the same time as the entire Vuelta peloton, who have arrived for their charter flight to the capital.

Seeing the riders in casual clothing makes you realise how skinny they are. Tracksuit trousers hang off bony hips and sag loosely around non-existent buttocks. Bare arms are marked by suntans and, in some cases, scabs.

As I leave security, I see Conor Dunne. At six foot eight he doesn't exactly blend in, although his frame has been eaten away by the effort of a three-week race just like the rest. He looks tired, dazed almost, but happy to know he will finish his first Grand Tour, even if it is in last place overall. After all, in order to finish last, you have to finish. When I catch up with him a few weeks after the Vuelta, he describes the experience of battling through. 'You're on the ropes – if you were boxing it'd be like guys punching you for round after round . . . '

I'm back home to watch the stage on television and smile at the reaction on social media when Froome has the temerity to defend his lead in the points competition as Team Sky tried to deny Trentin points at the intermediate sprint and then Froome sprinted for an eventual eleventh place at the line. Opinion seems to be split into two roughly unequal camps – some think it's fair game, others think it's unseemly of the overall winner to deny a sprinter. I wonder what it would have been like if Twitter had been around when Eddy Merckx used to win everything? At the end of the day, it's a bike race, people, not a holiday camp . . .

18. ADIOS, EL PISTOLERO

Fran Reyes

Alberto Contador, Pédaleur de Charme

It is 2am on 9 September 2017, and I am walking back to my hotel in Gijón through soft rain. At the same time five hundred kilometres away, Manel gives a concert in Madrid, where the Vuelta a España will finish in just over a day's time. Manel is not a person but a music band – a Catalan one that has managed to make its music popular outside its home region.

A friend of mine sends me a video from the show, with the band playing one of their most memorable hits, 'Boomerang'. This is a beautiful, rather melancholic song about the frustration of a young boy who struggles to impress girls during his summer vacations:

It was long ago, on that July when Indurain blew
and we all cursed that Danish guy and the slopes of Hautacam.

But tonight in Madrid the band put 'Big Mig' aside and alter the lyrics to pay homage to Contador.

My friend, not a fanatical cycling fan but someone with a passing interest, also sent me a text: 'Man, I am getting to admire Contador again. He is in that can't-be-fucked mood and seems to care little about the outcome of his attacks. I know you the purists might not like it and think it is a bit of a show, but it makes people like me turn the TV on. I am looking forward to see what he comes up with today on the Angliru.'

That positive test – let's call it the clenbuterol thing, that 'zero-comma-zero-zero-zero-zero-zero-zero-zero-zero-zero-zero-five' (50 picograms) – really boosted Alberto Contador's popularity in Spain. It was not as if he was unknown: after all, he had won three Tours de France with a style of climbing that harked back to Pedro Delgado. After Delgado, Miguel Indurain was the last Spanish cycling idol. 'Chaba' Jiménez came close, but Joseba Beloki, Alejandro Valverde and Óscar Freire didn't quite capture the collective imagination. Contador did, but to a lesser extent.

He operated in a crowded market. Contador's peak years, 2007–2010, coincided with a remarkable purple patch for Spanish sport. FC Barcelona and Real Madrid, as well as enjoying a fierce rivalry, were the best football clubs in Europe. The Spanish national team, known as 'La Roja', was the best in the world. Pau Gasol was leading a prodigious generation of basketball players. Fernando Alonso lured Spanish sports fans in their millions into watching Formula One. Rafa Nadal was the perfect athlete, the role model everyone would love as a brother or son-in-law. Who was Alberto Contador in this company? Just another champion standing on top of a podium enveloped in a red and yellow flag.

And then he met disaster.

The moment that best defines what those picograms of clenbuterol meant for Contador in terms of notoriety came four days after the news of his positive test. It was late September 2010 and the world's top riders were in Geelong, Australia, for the World Championships. Except for Contador, who sat on a sofa in front of Jordi González, one of Spain's most popular TV hosts, and Miguel Ángel Revilla, a politician. Revilla was from the northern region of Cantabria and a fixture on television – from news programmes to chat shows – thanks to his naïve, populist style and his down-to-earth personality. They were on *La Noria*, a live chat show aired at prime time every Saturday night. Contador was brought on stage at midnight for an interview about his positive test.

'The other day I saw you at the press conference, and I believed you,' Revilla said, addressing Contador. 'But, Jordi,' he added, turning to the host, 'with all due respect, I would like to do something. Alberto, can I ask you a question?'

'Yes, of course,' Contador quickly replied with a forced smile.

'Because, Jordi, you know, if I have a quality, that is psychology. And it is not because I have studied it – I just gained [an understanding of it] over the years. People say: "Revilla, you are always right." And I am right because I look people in the eye. I never look down to the floor. I look people in the eye.'

The camera pans out and we see three men sitting on a sofa in front of a live audience of maybe two hundred people. Watching on TV, meanwhile, are another six million Spaniards.

'Alberto, look me in the eye,' Revilla says, getting up and approaching Contador. 'Please: straight in the eye.' With a clumsy hand the politician grabs Contador's forearm. 'Have you doped?'

'No.'

'I believe you. This process is not going to be easy for you, but I believe you. And I'm sure that, at this moment, the whole of Spain is believing you.'

The audience went crazy, clapping and cheering. And you can be sure that many of the six million at home reacted the same way, believing in that instant that Contador was being unfairly treated – that he was a victim.

Embarking on a series of TV and radio appearances, on shows that weren't sports related, did wonders for Contador's image and profile. The stain of a doping ban was countered with a narrative that resonated with Spain's own sense of victimhood. This is a country that has been losing and becoming a lesser version of itself for four centuries; one whose people have suffered at the hands of corrupt leaders and foreign agents; one where heroes have usually been those savvy and courageous enough to confront those in power. The Don Quixote type, the tragic idol that alone and out of his mind fights against windmills thinking they are giants he shall slay, is attractive to the average Spaniard.

Contador was indisputably the world's greatest Grand Tour rider before his positive test. And he still managed, in the second act of his career following his suspension, some astounding performances – the 2012 Vuelta a España and the 2015 Giro d'Italia stand out. And then there was the way he influenced every race he took part in, the fear and the respect he seemed to arouse in his rivals, again an enchanting prospect for a country with an inferiority complex so deeply ingrained.

The way he turned things upside down on the Galibier at the 2011 Tour de France, making Andy Schleck miss what turned out to be his best-ever shot of winning the Tour (on the road, at least). How he caught out Team Sky on the way to Formigal at the 2016 Vuelta a España, a move that allowed Nairo Quintana to defeat Froome. Then, in 2017, came his attack with Mikel Landa in his last Tour de France, where he created a scenario in which the Basque climber could bite Froome's hand and, perhaps, challenge for the *maillot jaune*. All those performances were not victories, but glorious chapters in Contador's story.

The only problem was that Spanish stories and legends typically end rather miserably for their protagonists. Don Quixote died on his bed, after recovering his sanity only to realise all his feats counted for nothing. Spanish heroes come out of their tales rather tired and defeated. There isn't a happy ending for them, only depressing decay.

In Andorra, on the third day of his final Vuelta, it looked like Contador's farewell was going to be too Spanish for his own good. He was unable to match the pace of his rivals and even struggled to hold the wheel of his *domestique* Peter Stetina on the climb of La Comella. He lost two and a half minutes in eleven kilometres. Pinned against the ropes, if not quite sprawled on the canvas, he was lost for an explanation. 'I don't know what happened,' he said.

And then he bounced back by attacking in ten out of the seventeen remaining stages. Most of his moves were unproductive, but all of them thrilled and raised the pulse. The fact he kept falling short – failing, just, to claim the victory his efforts deserved – only heightened the sense of anticipation, raising excitement levels to a point where Manel were moved to change the lyrics of one of their most acclaimed songs to praise him, and this friend of mine was looking forward to the fireworks he might ignite on that final Angliru stage.

And what Contador produced was the apotheosis of his race craft – the skill that actually defines him best. The descent of El Cordal is one of the most daredevil examples in the Iberian Peninsula: merciless steep slopes, sharp corners hidden behind foliage and walls, irregular and usually wet tarmac. It has broken a lot of clavicles and even some careers. Contador launches his attack here, where it is more dangerous to accelerate and nobody will dare follow. The moment he catches the breakaway and the promising young Spaniards, Enric Mas and Marc Soler, who both co-operate with him despite racing for rival teams, has a passing-of-the-torch component. They can't stay with Contador; he reaches the steepest slopes of the Angliru alone. His all-out way of tackling the latest addition to the inventory of mythical climbs of the Vuelta a España resounds with that image of Don Quixote tilting at those windmills.

Only this time the hero manages to slay the giant. The Angliru is no Hautacam and there are no Danish or British guys to curse. Contador gets to perform a fairy-tale ending that, with him being an archetypal Spanish icon, feels somehow perfect in its imperfection.

For captions, see page 252

19. A SORT-OF REVIEW OF THE CYCLING YEAR, PART 2

Richard Moore, Lionel Birnie and Daniel Friebe

Back at the British Film Institute Café, on a day when the sky has turned dark . . .

RM: I imagine Tom Dumoulin is a lot of people's rider of the year but who's your most disappointing rider of the year?

DF: Ooff. I think it's possibly a little unfair to say Nairo Quintana, although . . .

RM: How many top-three placings in World Tour races did Quintana have?

DF: Including individual stages?

RM: No.

DF: One? The Giro?

RM: Two – he won Tirreno–Adriatico.

DF: Maybe not so disappointing, then. No, I think Quintana is a rider who's been slightly miscast at times. I think people expect Pantani-esque . . .

LB: Everyone is thinking of the Tour stage to Semnoz above Annecy at the end of the 2013 Tour . . .

RM: Or Alpe d'Huez in 2015 . . .

DF: Or Lagos de Covadonga in the 2016 Vuelta . . .

RM: So he's done it a few times! [laughs] Everyone's thinking of all these amazing performances and unfairly expecting him to do them again . . . so unfair!

LB: But I think he's more Rigoberto Urán than Luis Herrera. He's a lightweight diesel rather than an explosive little, um, um . . .

DF: Um.

LB: What am I thinking of?

DF: If you'd told anyone at Movistar that you'd get to the end of 2017 with questions about Quintana, and should he even be the leader, you would say that has to be a disappointing season. My mind goes back to an interview with Giovanni Visconti, who is no longer riding for Movistar, at the Giro, with *Corriere della Sera* newspaper, saying what a difficult leader Quintana is to ride for. He's taciturn, doesn't communicate much, there's an atmosphere in the team when he's leading that's not necessarily pleasant to be around, and Nibali was a lot – you could breathe fresh, clear air when he was around because you always knew exactly where you stood.

RM: Some farewells this year. You almost forget Tom Boonen, who retired after Paris–Roubaix. Thomas Voeckler. Alberto Contador – his popularity grew in defeat. Tyler Farrar. Manuel Quinziato. Andrew Talansky, who is probably the most surprising – twenty-eight years old. Touted as the next great American talent, won the Dauphiné in 2014, the high water mark of his career. Obviously very physically talented, not an easy guy to interview at all. A difficult guy by all accounts. I get the impression with the changing of the guard in that team, Cannondale–Drapac, that he's one of those riders who couldn't accept performing a supporting role, which would probably be required of him in the future.

LB: During the Tour I'm not sure he did perform a supporting role for Urán. He wasn't up there in crucial parts of mountain stages with Urán and Pierre Rolland. All three at their best, that would have been a formidable triumvirate. But Talansky never really lived up to that result at the Dauphiné, and the way he won it – it was a really pugnacious victory. But the problem for an American is that result is never going to be enough. The question is always, can you transfer that to the Tour de France? And that's kind of unfair. I'd say at best he's a sixth to tenth in a Grand Tour.

DF: A very courageous decision when you consider that even if his career hadn't lived up to the promise we thought it had, he would have been earning, I'm sure, upwards of three to four hundred thousand euros a year. Only twenty-eight, he's coming back in triathlon, but he will not be earning that kind of money in triathlon. So I think he deserves some credit for knowing that his heart wasn't in professional racing any more.

RM: How will Voeckler be remembered?

DF: For two Tours de France primarily: 2004, when he soared to prominence as a young rider, had the yellow jersey for ten, eleven days; gritty, courageous, not particularly easy on the eye as a rider. In a period when French cycling didn't really have a lot to shout about, he gave the home crowd some interest in the Tour de France – he was their main source of interest in the Tour de France. Then in 2011 one of the most amazing underdog performances in recent memory. The closest we've come, if you discount Oscar Perreiro in 2006, to what we'd call a Roger Walkowiak Tour de France. Walkowiak won the Tour de France in 1956 as a result . . . I don't think it's too unfair to say that it was largely thanks to a rogue breakaway and I hope that we'll see that happen again at some point in the Tour de France. In 2011 [Voeckler] didn't gain much time in a break but he was probably only a slightly smarter tactic on the Alpe d'Huez stage away from finishing on the podium, and could maybe even have won the 2011 Tour de France.

RM: Roger Walkowiak of course died this year as well. Reading some of the coverage of his death, he was quite bitter that he didn't get more credit for winning the Tour de France. We'd like to see another one like that, a surprise winner of the Tour de France. It's got to happen at some point.

LB: If Voeckler had won it would have been dismissed or written off as a fluke. Which is perverse, because the idea is to ride around France in the quickest time possible and if you gain time in an unexpected break, those seconds count just as much as seconds gained at the top of Alpe d'Huez.

RM: That first Tour I saw, in 1990, Chiappucci gained ten minutes and LeMond chipped away at it over three weeks . . .

DF: These *échappés fleuves* as the French call them, they do arrive at intervals of about one a decade. In 2001 Andre Kivilev came not too far away from upsetting the apple cart . . .

LB: It's going to take somebody racing in a way other than the accepted blueprint. Not to take anything away from Sunweb's performance at the Giro, they followed the same template: you get your guy in the lead then you ride together in a block in defence of that lead. There doesn't seem to be the room . . .

RM: How would you do it Lionel, if you were a DS?

LB: I'd do exactly the same because it's the most effective way of winning the race, of course. But as viewers, I personally would like to see someone come up with something different.

RM: I remember interviewing Shane Sutton in 2009 at the world track championships in Pruszkow and he said, 'You will not see Team Sky riding as a block on the front of the bunch. We're going to race in a completely different way, going to take a lot of our track stuff on to the road.'

LB: Well a lot of teams have come along and said they're going to do things differently and there are glimpses of a different approach; HTC–High Road, they targeted sprint wins; Cervélo did that, not as effectively . . .

RM: Orica sometimes . . .

LB: I suppose the closest to the kind of freelancing, attacking, swash-buckling rider is Vincenzo Nibali, because so often he has to do things on his own. Particularly at the Vuelta, we saw him trying something against all the odds . . . if he was four or five years younger you'd imagine Bahrain–Merida would build a train of riders around him. Because that's what everyone does. We're beginning to see the same thing at Orica: they're going to put more climbing resources behind Chaves and the two Yates brothers. That's the way you do it. I'm not a tactical genius. I'm no Paul Köchli.* But I'd like to see something different.

RM: Well, I think we've wrapped up the cycling year . . .

LB: Without even mentioning Peter Sagan's wins . . .

---

* DS at the La Vie Claire team in the 1980s.

RM: Oh yeah, he won the World Championship, didn't he. We talked in the podcast about his ability to win a race for which there is no formula, or blueprint, where you have to adapt yourself to unexpected, unusual conditions.

DF: He has to win Milan–San Remo.

RM: Paris–Roubaix?

DF: I'm not sure he'll ever win Paris–Roubaix.

LB: This is going to get written down in an actual book that will actually exist. It's not like a podcast, where nobody will go back and check.

RM: You speak about legacy, and Voeckler – the huge crowds around his bus at the Tour this year, yet what did he actually win? And the same with Sagan – for all his talent his palmarès is not reflective of the rider we think he is. He needs a few more major wins.

DF: He has to pull his finger out, doesn't he!

RM: So, chaps, we're almost at the end of the book. Have you enjoyed it, Lionel?

LB: I've loved it, we've relived the whole year. Now we're ready to start a new one.

RM: Well, yeah, almost.

RM: Daniel, have you enjoyed reading the book?

DF: It's been fine, yeah.

RM: F- fine? Wonderful. That's great.

LB: 'Fine.' So effusive!

RM: But it's a moment to reflect – we've gone full circle, from all starting out as writers, branching out into podcasting, spreading our wings in audio, then returning to writing with a book about a podcast. A strange development, in a way, but Lionel, if you recall the origins of the podcast, you were quite a reluctant convert initially.

LB: Well, I was because you sprung it on me on my birthday, after we'd opened a bottle of champagne to celebrate, if you remember. We were in, er . . . [laughs]

RM: We did that in reverse as well – celebrated the podcast before we'd even started recording it.

LB: I used to get very concerned about background noise when we were recording in bars. We seemed to have a knack of arriving to record a podcast at the Tour de France at a bar just as the waiter was clearing up two hundred glasses and plates . . .

RM: Or just as a lorry started reversing on the street outside the bar . . . very atmospheric.

LB: Yeah, but it was very homespun in those days. You guys pre-dated *The Cycling Podcast* and I'm a new signing in many ways because you two . . .

RM: Yeah, Daniel, we were pioneers, weren't we, 2008, 2009?

DF: We were podcasting about Lucien Petit-Breton and Fausto Coppi when they were doing their thing in the Tour de France.

LB: I remember listening to your Fausto Coppi podcast back in '52. It was excellent.

RM: It was the first time TV pictures – was it not the first time the race was broadcast live on TV, Alpe d'Huez, 1952, with Fausto Coppi?

DF: You are right.

RM: But it wasn't podcasted, that came fifty or so years later, but there have been two waves. In that first wave, 2008/09, we didn't have much of a sense of there being an audience out there for podcasts. I think the smartphone revolution has done a lot to enable people to get podcasts. But I don't think any of us could have imagined that the podcast would become one of the main things that we do, and certainly for us, Lionel, when we go to the Tour de France, it's the only thing we do.

LB: Yeah, I mean, in 2012 we were both working for a magazine, *Cycle Sport*, and Daniel was working for another magazine, *Procycling*, and I think we all had newspaper work at the time as well, and the podcast you sprung on me was just a conversation about the day's stage or a couple of stages, because I don't think we did one every day, recorded on your iPhone and uploaded to the internet. I've just looked up how many were listening and if the two or three of you who were listening to that podcast are out there reading this don't go and revisit them because I'm not sure they were all that good, were they?

RM: I doubt it, and if they are still there, I hope they'll be erased soon.

DF: There was one memorable highlight from that era of the podcast, the prehistory of the podcast. I can still remember where we were sitting. This tells you how glamorous it was then – we were sitting on a football pitch outside the sports hall where the press room was located on that particular day. Anyway, Richard and I had a blazing row about patriotism, or my lack of patriotism. LIVE!

RM: That was quite a recurring theme, I remember, in the early days.

DF: There was one in particular where it got quite incendiary.

RM: Yeah, I think that when we started off, Daniel, especially in the old one, the *Procycling* one, in 2008, it was set up to be quite adversarial where there'd be something we'd have to debate. Whereas I think our podcast, I hope, is more conversational, and more about insight than opinion, he says hopefully . . .

LB: We keep all the blazing arguments off air, don't we? We're a bit more professional these days, maybe?

The first Tour de France for *The Cycling Podcast* was in 2013 and we were the *Humans Invent Cycling Podcast* and we were supported by Sharp. The three of us got together in central London to record a Tour de France preview and we sat in a park on a sunny afternoon a week or so before the Tour . . .

RM: Hyde Park.

LB: And then I didn't go to Corsica because I missed the Grand Départ, I went to the Glastonbury festival instead, clearly not anticipating what a great success *The Cycling Podcast* would turn out to be. I decided I didn't need to be there at the start of it all. So you two were in charge for the opening weekend and I listened to all the episodes on the flight down to Nice and Ciro Scognamiglio made his first appearance. I was not entirely sure that we hadn't broken *The Cycling Podcast* before I'd even managed to get to the Tour. He was so extraordinary and just not what I was expecting to hear and I think that was when I first realised that one of the strengths of podcasting was that we did not have the same constraints of publishing in the written word. We have experimented a bit over the years – we haven't been too avant-garde – but we have been able to push ourselves and try different things. It certainly feels a freer form of media than writing. Certainly that first Tour, in 2013, when I was balancing written work with podcasting I found that recording the podcast was incredibly enjoyable, and the part of the day I looked forward to most. I'd go back to the press room to start on my written work – and I am not saying that there isn't a place for written journalism, of course there is, there will always be a place for good written journalism, it will always exist and the best of it will always have the power to capture the imagination – but having ruminated on the events of the stage with you two and knowing that my thoughts and the stuff that I'd worked on over the course of the day was already out there in an audio form, I'd sit down at my computer and it felt like wading through treacle to do it all again in a less immediate form. That's not to denigrate the written word at all, but it showed me at that time there was a lot more potential in the audio format.

RM: One thing that struck me – and I think, Daniel, you'd agree – was that we seemed to form a different relationship with those who listen to the podcast than with those who read our stuff. It's different, isn't it, a different kind of connection that's made.

DF: Yeah, I would say so and I think over the past fifteen, twenty years we've seen a phenomenon – this ubiquity of information, this democratisation of information. There's so much about professional cycling now compared to when we all started following it, whether that was twenty or thirty years ago, when information was quite hard to come by. I think with that, and particularly in the UK where there's been a lot of success, people have become more and more focused on racing and the actual intricacies of that at the expense of a lot of the décor and the things that make cycling unique; by that I mean the context in which it happens – the place, the sounds, the flavours – all things we're able to articulate with the podcast. These are things that I think are neglected and taken for granted now. The colour stories – the man in the beret at the side of the road, drinking his pastis – were maybe things that Channel 4 in the UK would once show an interest in, say, in the 1980s, when they felt that people didn't know that much about the racing. Now, though, the traditional media almost assume that everyone knows what the Tour and other races are about and therefore focus on the nitty gritty of the racing. This leaves us to perhaps remind people what a unique spectacle it is outside of the sporting aspects.

RM: I enjoy the balance that we're at least able to strive for in the podcast between the serious stuff that goes on in pro cycling – doping and so on – and the humour, and some of the outlandish characters that abound in this sport. We can seem to strike that balance more easily in the podcast than in the written word, I don't know why that is, but we certainly try to find some humour, don't we.

Another thing I've enjoyed has been expanding what we do, and learning about how podcasts work, and don't work, and how you can tell stories differently in audio. Our friends specials, which we started in 2015 and can be more like documentary-style episodes, have certainly stretched us, and allowed us to be a bit more ambitious – and we owe a big debt of thanks to our talented producers, who have held our hands at times. The live shows have been another expansion of what we do – taking the podcast on the road, so to speak. That's both incredibly nerve-racking and terrifying, and also hugely enjoyable and rewarding, and a highlight for me was our show at the Arts Theatre in London's West End at the end of 2017. Almost the whole *Cycling Podcast* 'family' was there – us three, plus Orla Chennaoui, François Thomazeau, Fran Reyes, Seb Piquet, Detective Inspector Rob Hatch of the Pronunciation Police . . . the only one missing was Ciro Scognamiglio, who had a prior engagement. He was at a Jamiroquai concert in Milan – a most Ciro thing to do. Our special guest was Matt White, the Orica–Scott DS, who is one of our regular go-to guys at races because he offers so much in terms of information and insight . . .

LB: I think that's why our coverage of the Grand Tours works the way it does. We capture the ups and downs of not only a three-week race but also the journey. I don't know about you two, but I've always found being away from

home for three weeks quite challenging – there is a sense of adventure and uncertainty and the excitement of seeing new places but also revisiting familiar ones. Every day there's the potential for something to go wrong. Remember at the Giro a couple of years ago, Rich, when we added a fifty-kilometre detour to our journey by taking the wrong motorway junction?

RM: I do. Also that when we tried to re-join the motorway at the next junction, to retrace our steps, we – well, I – took the wrong slip road and added another thirty kilometres.

LB: Some of the hotels can be rustic, which is a polite word for bloody awful, or downright weird. Dinner time, which as you know is an important part of my day, can vary from the sublime to the inedible. I think it took a little while for us to have the confidence to try to capture some of the sounds and flavours of being at the Grand Tours but when we did the reaction was so positive. I remember going out to the cobbles at the 2014 Tour de France and our producer Jon Moonie put together a piece from the random collection of stuff I'd recorded as I watched the race go by and the effect was that it transported the listeners to the roadside . . .

DF: Though it also ruined a new pair of Adidas Gazelle trainers, Napalm . . .

LB: The sacrifice was worth it. The year before that, I remember feeling that we'd made a bit of a breakthrough during the 2013 Tour when we started getting complaints on Twitter that the episode titles were giving away who had won the stage and I thought, people are actually listening to this. When Dan Martin won in the Pyrenees we hit 10,000 downloads for the first time and we'd only been going a week, and I thought, there might be something in this.

But even now there are people who will say, 'What's a podcast?' and I explain that it's basically a radio show that you can listen to at any time. We've been lucky that some people saw something in what we were doing and chose to support us. Sharp got us going, of course, and when the 2013 Tour de France finished, I thought that would be it for another year but people got in touch asking us to carry on and so we persuaded Sharp to support us enough to keep a weekly show going.

RM: Then in 2016 Science in Sport came on board. Without them, we'd not have been able to go to the Giro d'Italia that year and replicate our Tour coverage – that was an important milestone for us. And then Rapha came in as title sponsor for the 2016 Tour de France and that – as well as the income from our valued friends of the podcast – has enabled us to cover all three of the Grand Tours and to launch *The Cycling Podcast Féminin*. I'd be the first to admit that I didn't follow women's racing very closely when Orla and I started that, and the feedback we've had suggests a lot of our listeners were in the same boat, but it means we've been on the same journey, getting to know the riders and races and, through that, developing a real interest.

Anyway, chaps, I'm afraid we have to wind this up. We've reached the end of our first book. Literally run out of pages. We hope you, the reader, have enjoyed it. Thank you, Daniel.

DF: Thank you, Rich.

RM: Thank you, Lionel.

LB: Thanks – see you next year.

GALLERY CAPTIONS

Simon Gill

CLASSICS GALLERY

Page 1

I had been to the velodrome in Roubaix before, for the finish of Paris–Roubaix in 2015 when John Degenkolb had won, but with all the activity going on I had not really taken a close look at the track. During the Lionel of Flanders, we rode over to Roubaix and I had the chance to do a few laps. The concrete surface is bumpy, cracked and quite dead to ride on, which surprised me a bit. I took a few photographs of the track, playing with the angles and the lines, then I spotted the daisies, which were a sure sign that spring had arrived. And spring in Roubaix means the Hell of the North.
Exposure: 1/8000
F: 5

Page 2-3

This photograph was taken on the main road that runs more or less parallel to the Oude Kwaremont during the GP E3. It's possible to shoot the leaders on the cobbles and then run across to catch some of the chasers on the fast descent. That stretch had some traumatic memories for me because it was the scene of a horrific hangover on my previous visit for Kuurne–Brussels–Kuurne when I was ambushed by some unexpectedly strong Belgian beers the night before. I remember lying down in my camper van, parked on the verge next to the descent, as the junior riders whizzed past. This time I was in peak condition and had an idea in mind. I used a pan flash technique to convey the speed. The flash has to be close for this technique to work, so I set up my wireless remote-controlled flash as close to the road as I could, then picked my vantage point and reacted as soon as I saw Peter Sagan's rainbow jersey. I had to pan across, matching Sagan's speed, to make the effect work and I was really pleased with the result.

Exposure: 1/40

F: 22

Page 4-5

The day before Ghent–Wevelgem we rode over to the Plugstreets, the gravel roads that were used in the race for the first time in 2017. The Belgian Classics are known for the cobbles so it was exciting to see something different. That particular section went past the field where the Christmas Day truce football match between German and British soldiers took place in 1914, which was being re-enacted by people in First World War uniforms. I walked back down the gravel road looking for a good spot. No one quite knew what effect the gravel would have, so I picked a gentle bend, not because I was hoping anyone would crash, but because I knew it would challenge the riders' bike-handling skills and might provoke some dynamic body shapes as they tackled the corner. I had no idea at that point that Greg Van Avermaet would eventually win the race, although I knew he was one of the favourites. It's always pleasing to find out who won and know you've got a good shot them in action.

Exposure: 1/4000

F: 8

Page 6-7

Every time I go to Flanders, or Paris–Roubaix, I can't help but focus on the cobbles. I think every photographer does. To me every stretch of cobblestones is different and I like playing around with the angles and the light. On the day of the Dwars Door Vlaanderen, we parked up at the finish, outside the football stadium in Waregem, and rode back down the course to the final stretch of cobbles. It's a street called Herlegemstraat and it's not a famous section by any means but it was where Yves Lampaert applied the pressure that would eventually win him the race.
Exposure: 1/3200
F: 6.3

Page 8

At the start of the Grand Prix E3 in Harelbeke, Peter Sagan was in a good mood. Dance music had been blasting out of the Bora–Hansgrohe bus for a good while before he emerged to cheers in his world champion's rainbow jersey. I also spotted Philippe Gilbert, the reigning Belgian champion, whose socks, in Belgian champion's colours of course, didn't quite cover the more permanent mark of the rainbow bands tattooed just above his ankle. It's a simple tattoo and perhaps not for everyone but I couldn't help wondering how long it took to ink five rings of solid colour round his leg, and how much it hurt?
Sagan:
Exposure: 1/1250
F: 5.6

Gilbert:
Exposure: 1/800
F: 6.3

GIRO GALLERY

Page 1

It was very warm and sunny at the start of stage 8 in Molfetta. As I walked from the team buses to the start line I crossed a little square and looked up to see all these pink umbrellas suspended in the air. There was something about the combination of the blue sky, the sunshine and the pink that captured the essence of the Giro d'Italia.
Exposure: 1/4000
F: 5

Page 2-3

Alberobello in the Puglia region is well known for these little conical roof buildings called trulli and I wanted to get up high so I could capture them. I was walking up the finish straight and I saw some people on a roof terrace. I waved to try to catch their eye and then I waved a ten euro note – which I hoped would be international sign-language for "can I take photographs from your terrace?" I've done this a few times, asked people if I can stand on their balconies and I always think it's polite to offer them something for a thank you drink. On this occasion, they offered me a beer and I grabbed one from the table, took a swig and realised in horror it was almost empty and it had a cigarette butt in it.
Exposure: 1/2000
F: 8

Page 4, top

Stage 5 to Messina took Vincenzo Nibali home. It was the last stage in Sicily before the ferry back to mainland Italy. There were a couple of

finishing laps around the town and I was looking for Nibali. The riders were approaching from over my shoulder and crossing a roundabout. I spotted him and as he passed a bit of space opened up around him. I was able to get him more or less alone in the shot. It would have been perfect if the 'Forza Nibali' sign painted on a bed sheet and hung from the balcony in the top right hand corner had been fully in shot. So close!
Exposure: 1/6400
F: 5.6

Page 4, bottom

Laurens ten Dam is surely the most dribbly rider in the peloton so it was great to catch him mid-dribble like this.
Exposure: 1/2500
F: 7.1

Page 5, top

This is the Montefalco time trial that went through the vineyards. I found a nice spot near where a big family was having a barbecue and enjoying the local wine. They offered me a glass and kept topping it up over the afternoon. Here, Geraint Thomas, who had crashed hard on the stage to Blockhaus a couple of days earlier, turned in an incredible ride to finish second to Tom Dumoulin. When the guy on the bike with the roll of carpet on his handlebars pulled up I shouted and waved at him to get out of my shot but in hindsight it makes the picture. What could be more normal than stopping to watch the Giro while taking a roll of carpet home?
Exposure: 1/2500
F: 8

Page 5, bottom

Thibaut Pinot going well on the Blockhaus climb (but not quite well enough to win the stage, that was Nairo Quintana). I set up a remote camera for this one. I carry three cameras and try to be three photographers at once but setting up the remote can be time consuming. I spent ages faffing about, walking up and down, setting the angle of the camera, checking what would be in the frame, trying to work out what line the riders would take as they came past. The nature of the remote is that there's a lot of luck involved but when it comes off you can get a shot you wouldn't have got any other way.
Exposure: 1/4000
F: 10

Page 6-7

The final climb to Peschici featured this very tight hairpin bend with about a kilometre to go. This is another remote shot because I'm actually in the photo (in the green bib next to the barriers in the centre of the hairpin bend). The four leaders flew into the corner so fast and Valerio Conti went down. You can almost tell from his body language that he's thinking about getting up as quickly as possible but knows in this split-second his chance has gone. Gorka Izagirre, the next rider in dark blue, was the eventual winner.
Exposure: 1/1000
F: 10

Page 8, top

Matteo Pelucchi on the Etna stage. The leaders had long gone and I was walking back to the finish line to meet Richard, Lionel and Daniel and I

spotted one rider coming towards me. When I see riders in this sort of state it reminds me how tough they are. (If this was me, I'd have stopped immediately, but they carry on – in Pelucchi's case, bandaged up for several more days.)
Exposure: 1/5000
F: 5

Page 8, bottom

In contrast to Pelucchi, Tom Dumoulin looks immaculate. He's far too photogenic for my liking – the camera loves him. The cheekbones, the pink jersey – this could have been a studio pose for a fashion shoot.
Exposure: 1/5000
F: 2

TOUR DE FRANCE GALLERY

Page 1

Geraint Thomas in yellow in Düsseldorf on the morning of the stage to Liège. He always seems relaxed before stage starts and happy to chat to people or stop for a photograph. Being in the yellow jersey didn't change that.
Exposure: 1/320
F: 4

Page 2-3

Stage 3 finished on a short hill so I walked down to the steepest section, with about 250m to go. As they came past, Peter Sagan turned on the after-burners and accelerated away to win. But it wasn't until dinner that evening, as I scrolled through the images on my camera between courses, that I realised Sagan had pulled his foot clean out of his pedal and I had *the* shot.

Exposure: 1/640

F: 6.3

Page 4-5

The Tour organisers and police stopped spectators from gathering in the barren, rocky section known as la Casse Déserte. I wandered down a bit and found a spot to myself and looked back up towards the summit. When the publicity caravan came past, I cleaned up because there were no fans to compete with, so I was fairly high on a sugary buzz of Haribo sweets by the time the race arrived. Warren Barguil came past alone, in the polka-dot jersey, on his way to the stage win. Initially I was disappointed that the motorbike was in the shot but later I came to appreciate its presence. Otherwise it could just be a rider out on a training ride. It was eerie and quiet on the Izoard, compared to the madness of the other mountain climbs, but the motorbike just over Barguil's shoulder, with the camera trained on him all the way, highlighted that the riders are never alone during the Tour de France.

Exposure: 1/1000

F: 9

Page 6-7

As if to contrast with the emptiness of the Izoard, this shot on the Col du Galibier shows how the fans cling to the mountains, craning their necks to get the best view. This section of road seems precariously carved into the edge of the rock and there was quite a drop down the other side. I

clambered across the rocky surface and caught Dan Martin, Chris Froome, Rigoberto Uran and Romain Bardet as they came through together.
Exposure: 1/400
F: 6.3

Page 8, top

These two pictures show the past and present of French cycling. In terms of popularity, Warren Barguil is taking over from the retiring Thomas Voeckler. The Barguil shot was taken on stage 15 as I returned to the race after a few days' holiday. It was weird returning to the race, knowing that it had continued in my absence the whole time. I had left it in Chambéry and headed to the airport in Marseille. While I'd been away, they'd trans-ferred over to the west of the country, headed through the Pyrenees and were back within a comfortable drive of Marseille again. Because I was aiming to meet the race on that Sunday wherever I could, there wasn't time to pick my spot. As it turned out, there was nothing picturesque so I used a long lens to capture Wawa in action.
Exposure: 1/3200
F: 6.3

Page 8, bottom

By the end of the Tour, the cheers for Barguil rivalled and sometimes exceeded those for Voeckler, although the veteran Frenchman remains extremely popular. This being his last Tour, he seemed very relaxed. Most mornings he was among the last riders to roll up to the start line. One morning he was so late the Tour almost went without him. In 2018, the Tour really will go without him.
Exposure: 1/4000
F: 7.1

VUELTA A ESPAÑA GALLERY

Page 1

Chris Froome walks onto the podium in Logroño after winning the stage 16 time trial.
Exposure: 1/1600
F: 4.8

Page 2-3

Alberto Contador in his final Vuelta a España, chasing Stefan Denifl on the climb to Los Machucos. As it turned out, his effort was in vain because Denifl held on to win the stage. I love this shot because Contador is giving it everything, the fans are excited, the young boy is getting a great view from his dad's shoulders and the Spanish flag sums up what Contador means to his supporters.
Exposure: 1/3200
F: 5

Page 4, top

This is in the final few metres of stage 18 to Santo Toribio de Liébana and Chris Froome is piling on the pressure, as the expression on Alberto Contador's face confirms. Little did we know that the urine sample Froome gave at the post-race anti-doping test would return an adverse analytic finding for excessive levels of his asthma medication, salbutamol.
Exposure: 1/1250
F: 6.3

As the riders approached the top of the Angliru at the end of the penultimate stage, they were all on the limit. The road is so steep at times it's almost possible to walk alongside the riders. It also means the riders are well spaced out so a great opportunity to capture an image of each of them suffering in isolation. Here are Bob Jungels (page 4, bottom) Michael Woods (page 5, top), and Fabio Aru (page 5, bottom).
All:
Exposure: 1/1250
F: 6.3

Page 6-7

The finish line shot of the winner crossing the line has almost no value for a freelance photographer these days because it is usually made available for free by the race organisers within minutes of the stage ending and before I've even got back to the press room it will have been published online dozens if not hundreds of times. So I try to find a different angle and in Gijon I waited until Thomas De Gendt had come past me and captured his victory salute.
Exposure: 1/1250
F: 3.5

Page 8

He didn't win the race but the 2017 Vuelta was all about Alberto Contador for a lot of people. It took him almost three weeks to get his stage win but he was in a good mood whenever I saw him. This is before the start of stage 18 in Suances.
Exposure: 1/800
F: 5

FINAL WORD

We have many people to thank, not only for helping with this book but also for enabling us to create and grow *The Cycling Podcast* to the extent that in 2017 we produced close to 150 episodes. We have a fabulous team of producers and other members of the extended *Cycling Podcast* family who contribute in different but essential ways.

Considerable thanks, then, are owed to Simon Gill for his incredible pictures and understated, but frequently hilarious, company; to Orla Chennaoui for her energy (balls) and for helping make such a success of *The Cycling Podcast Féminin*; to François Thomazeau, Fran Reyes, Ciro Scognamiglio and Sebastien Piquet, not only for contributing chapters to this book but for providing interesting, and fun, company on our travels; to Ashleigh Moolman Pasio, Joe Dombrowski and many of the other riders who have given time to *The Cycling Podcast* (and in some cases even listen to it, and tell us what they think of it); to David Luxton, our agent and counsellor, as well as his *domestique de luxe*, Nick Walters, and road captain, Rebecca Winfield; to Jonathan Rowe, who oils our wheels; to Nick Christian, who pens our witty weekly newsletter; and to those producers who iron out and add sparkle to our ramblings: Alexandra Adey, Adam Bowie, Matt Field, Jon Moonie, Will Jones, Paul Scoins and Tom Whalley. Thanks, too, to the sponsors who have supported us since 2013 – they showed imagination, if nothing else, in getting behind a podcast – and especially to our current backers, Rapha and Science in Sport, whose support goes way beyond helping fund so many free podcasts. Almost finally, thanks to Tim Broughton of Yellow Jersey Press, who saw the potential for turning sounds in your ear into words on a page.

*

And to you, the listener (or reader), we say a huge thank you. The podcast has grown organically since those scratchy, stumbling, recorded-on-an-iPhone early days, and our audience has grown with us, in every sense. Some of you are paid-up Friends of the Podcast (receiving exclusive, and we like to think rather special, episodes), and to you we are extremely grateful. To you all, we have been sustained by your support and encouragement, we have learned and, we hope, improved thanks to your feedback, and we are constantly amazed by and grateful for your loyalty and sense of kinship with the podcast. We hope you have enjoyed our journey through the cycling year and look forward to sharing another one with you next year, and beyond.

Richard Moore, Lionel Birnie and Daniel Friebe
The Cycling Podcast

EST.1998

Yellow Jersey Press celebrates 20 years of quality sports writing

Yellow Jersey Press launched in 1998, with *Rough Ride*,
Paul Kimmage's William Hill Sports Book of the Year. In those
early days, the Yellow Jersey list sought to give a platform to
brilliant stories, which happened to be framed within a sporting
environment. Over the past two decades, its name has become
synonymous with quality sports writing, covering all sports from
the perspective of player, professional observer and passionate fan.

Sport is about more than simple entertainment. It represents
a determination to challenge and compete. It binds individuals
with a common goal, and often reflects our experiences in the
wider world. Yellow Jersey understands this as much as its readers.

This edition was first published in the
Yellow Jersey Press 20th Anniversary Year.

@YellowJersey_ed